Early Praise for *Eyes Wide Open*

"OneHope27's *Eyes Wide Open* delivers on the title's promise by revealing the joy and heartbreak of foster care utilizing the interactions with some of the children placed in their director's care, their parents, social workers, other foster parents, her family and extended support team. Shared in story form, the pages are filled with the kind of grace and truth needed to bring hope and healing to children and families involved in the foster care system."

- Shelly Radic, President of Project 1.27

"Walking through a field of tall grass is easier when someone before you has worn a path for you to follow. *Eyes Wide Open* is an honest and transparent narrative that shows the way to caring well for kids and families in foster care."

- Jason Weber, National Director of Foster Care Initiatives, Christian Alliance for Orphans

"This book is an incredible resource for anyone considering engaging in foster care. She generously shares her family's experiences with a vulnerable honesty, revealing both the joys and the painful realities. She also clears up many of the prevalent, and harmful, misconceptions associated with foster care."

- Scott Kingston, Co-Director of Welcomed

"In *Eyes Wide Open*, Charonne Ganiere has invited us into the depths of her and her family's own personal experience with caring for kids from hard places and challenged us with grace, humility, and strength to consider the unique implications for our own lives as well. If you are exploring the possibility of getting involved with foster care, or are already involved in this profoundly difficult yet rewarding place, then this book is a must read for you. You'll find the insight, encouragement, and hope you need no matter where you are on your journey."

- Jason Johnson, author of *ReFraming Foster Care*, *Everyone Can Do Something*, and jasonjohnsonblog.com

"Practical, powerful insight to help smooth the path and prepare the hearts of those considering the foster care and adoption journey!"

- Scott Murrish, Ambassador of Vision, Royal Family KIDS

EYES WIDE OPEN

An Educational Resource About Foster Care
and the People We Met Along the Way Who Changed Us

OneHope27 with Charonne Ganiere

Orange Hat Publishing
www.orangehatpublishing.com - Waukesha, WI

Eyes Wide Open
An Educational Resource About Foster Care
and the People We Met Along the Way Who Changed Us
Copyright © 2018 OneHope27 with Charonne Ganiere
ISBN 978-1-948365-27-7

Eyes Wide Open
An Educational Resource About Foster Care
and the People We Met Along the Way Who Changed Us
by OneHope27 with Charonne Ganiere

For information, please contact:

Orange Hat Publishing
www.orangehatpublishing.com
603 N Grand Ave, Waukesha, WI 53186

Cover design by Kevin Ganiere

www.orangehatpublishing.com

For anyone who has fostered, is considering foster care, or is connected to a foster family. This resource is for you.

Contents

Foreword

When I was nine, my parents told my sister and me they had become foster parents and we were about to get two brothers. The boy's biological sister, and now my sister, later joined our family as well. That first night, on our old navy and green striped couch, one part of my family's story began. I didn't know that foster care would be part of my professional life, and I didn't know what I would learn, how I would love, or how I would hurt because of my parents' call to grow our family. Charonne's stories are for anyone who wants a preview about how foster care is going to change you.

People ask me a lot about what it was like to grow up as a biological kid in a family with kids from foster care. Most of the time, prospective foster parents who already have children seem to ask as a way to make sure they aren't going to screw up their biological kid. I don't think my answers are ever satisfactory. When I found out that brothers were coming, I was ecstatic. Not for any holy reason, but because my sister and I fought all of the time and I thought brothers would be more fun. I remember the day one of my brothers was adopted. I remember laying on benches outside the courtroom, bored, waiting for the judge. The hearing was short. I don't remember what was said even though I remember knowing that it was special, but I remember not feeling any different afterward. He was already my brother.

After the hearing, my parents took us out to celebrate at an arcade and go-kart place that we normally didn't go to because it was expensive. I wondered why we were celebrating another day in this way. Now I know that my parents were marking what was an important and beautiful day, but I didn't care. Instead, I marched up to my dad and asked him if we were going to do this every year. Because this *was* like a birthday, and just because my brother was adopted didn't mean that he deserved two birthdays. I wasn't a saint. I was a sister who pranked and picked on my siblings until they were bigger than me. When people ask me about my childhood, my answers aren't extraordinary because my childhood wasn't special. It was life.

At the time, I didn't understand what my parents had been through during their foster care journey. I didn't know about appeals, termination of parental rights, the other court hearings, and the many meetings and calls with social workers. I knew about some of it, but it wasn't until I was older and working professionally with other parents through their foster care journeys that I understood why every adoption and every reunification deserved to be celebrated and also grieved. I now understand that when my siblings came to us, we celebrated our new family, but also needed to grieve the fracture of another. And I now know that reunifications are the most desired outcome of foster care, celebrating that a family can be made whole while also recognizing that there is a foster family missing that child's presence in their home.

Despite not having the holiest approach to foster care as a child, I now see how much watching my parents open our home and growing our family has taught me about the nature of God and the way we're called to live. These lessons, unbeknownst to me or my parents for quite some time, shaped who I am today. After reading Charonne's story, I was surprised by how many of our lessons seemed to overlap.

When I tell my parents about the things I learned from them, they are surprised. They were just doing what God asked them to do, to them it was just the right thing to do. Like Charonne and Kevin, my parents wanted to parent kids who needed parents. This was the first lesson for me—God uses the boringly ordinary.

This idea of God using the ordinary has become slightly cliché. When I look at people I admire who claim to be ordinary, I perceive a sense of false humility. To me, they so clearly aren't ordinary, and I begin to think the things they do are beyond my reach or capacity. I see people do this frequently in the foster care world. "Oh, I could never do that" is a refrain everyone who is familiar with child welfare hears over and over. But here's the thing. We were a family with a stay-at-home mom, two kids, and a dog—we were just missing the white picket fence. My parents didn't have a background in ministry or child development. They were boringly ordinary. But God asked them to do something extraordinary, and they took the first step, and then the step after that, and then the one after that. They weren't perfect, they messed up (they would agree with me), but they just took one ordinary step at a time. When we label someone as extraordinary we think they have something we don't. It's not true. Sometimes that's self-doubt, and sometimes it's the thing we say to ourselves to feel less guilty about saying no. Perhaps the saying should be changed to, "God uses the boringly ordinary when those who are boringly ordinary trust God."

Trust—that was the second lesson I learned. In foster care, you have to make hard decisions, and sometimes you have to make life-altering, potentially trauma-causing decisions. Charonne's vulnerability in describing some of the decisions she and Kevin faced is admirable. These are the decisions foster care recruitment organizations don't put on brochures, but I assure you that at some point, every foster parent, my parents included, have made decisions like these. I watched my parents walk through these, and I watched my parents trust God for themselves and for my siblings. Churches talk about trust frequently, but too often we trust God with our salvation and then ensure we never put ourselves in situations where we would have to trust God for anything difficult. Fostering and serving vulnerable families puts almost every aspect of your life into God's hands—your home, your money, your marriage, your kids, your time . . . the list goes on. In particular, I think foster care (and anytime you care for someone) tests your trust in two unique areas. First, do you trust God with your emotional health? Second, are you ready to trust God with the life of someone you love?

When my parents welcomed children from foster care into our home, it turned out to be just the start of my journey. Outside of my job at DC127, a nonprofit mobilizing churches around foster care in Washington, DC, I've mentored a young woman who was in, and has now aged, out of foster care. I've also walked with a mom whose children were at risk of entering foster care, periodically caring for the children. I've learned that to trust God with your time is to trust God with your emotional health. We think that our emotional health depends on our ability to find space in life—to take pauses, rests, and vacations. But when you foster a child or walk with someone who is in crisis, it becomes a twenty-four seven role. While rest and pauses are necessary (and if you know a foster parent, go babysit for them), you're just not going to be able to take as many breaks as you need. You have to trust God to help you mentally and physically carry things beyond your ability. When a foster parent welcomes another child into an already full home, they do this because they know the need and they are trusting that God will provide the rest.

The second lesson of trust has been the hardest for me. In walking with these two amazing and strong young women, they and their children have become family to me. As they have generously opened up their lives to me, I've seen how systems are working against them, and I've seen the barriers they are working to overcome. When you love someone, you want to fix everything for them. As it turns out, that's not possible. You can't undo trauma, instantly take racism out of systems, or unbreak broken families. While yes, you can learn about trauma-informed care, advocate against unjust policies, and provide a stable family to bring others into, these are actions that take time. But on the individual level, when someone you love is in the middle of a painful situation, you will never be able to address all of it. You do what you can, but there will always come a point where what you can provide will fall short of what they need. In that moment, are you ready to trust God with their life and their future? It doesn't mean everything is going to be okay, and it doesn't mean you ever stop working for those long-term hopes, but it does mean that you trust the situation and the person you love to a God who is bigger than any trauma, system, and brokenness. Charonne's stories about the children who left her home in ways that didn't feel complete resonated deeply with me. She had to trust that God would be present in that child's journey even when she was not. This trust is difficult, but it reminds us that we were never meant to be anyone's savior, but we are meant to point them to one.

Finally, while my parents taught me a lot, my siblings also taught me so much. If any of the four of you are reading this, I am incredibly grateful for each of you in my life. My siblings have taught me a lot about love. They have each forgiven me after I deeply hurt them, and I have seen them take the high road when people treat them unfairly. At the core of all of this, they are my brothers and sisters. And while I'm a little cooler than them for being the oldest, we're on the same plane. We're peers. I've heard some well-meaning comments that imply that anyone who fosters is saint-like for helping kids who desperately need the help. I think this is indicative of a larger approach to things we label as "outreach," "service," or "missions." These words often imply that we are in one place and the people we are serving are in another. I've fallen into this trap over and over. Too many times in life I have approached someone thinking that the knowledge, goods, and message I was bringing would in some way save them. At its core, this thinking is about a transaction. Foster care is about relationships. And in any true relationships, especially as Christians, we will inevitably be reminded that our "child of God" status isn't any higher than anyone else's. We're peers, and we're siblings.

At DC127, we say that we'll never change the rhythms of our city unless we change the rhythms of our lives. This means that if we want to change the brokenness that families and kids in our city experience, we have to change the way we live. Loving our neighbor is loving our brother and our sister, and that's a way of life. Love for others can't be in silos or single actions; rather, when we decide to live a life that is focused on loving God and loving others, it changes the way we work, live, parent, commute, and rest. And when we do that, the people we love are no longer people we serve, but family. They become our brothers and our sisters, and we learn that they always were.

Charonne's stories give us a picture of what can happen when we trust God and decide to live a life that is focused on loving others. She bravely gives us a seat at her kitchen table, sharing the joys, hurts, and lessons of fostering. She doesn't shy away from sharing the tensions that come with fostering, and these are things that prospective foster homes need to hear and current foster parents will be encouraged by. Fostering can be isolating, and by sharing these stories, Charonne reminds other foster parents that they are not alone, they are not the only ones carrying these burdens, and that even in the hardest moments, there can be hope.

Chelsea Geyer, Executive Director of DC127
(dc127.org/)

Introduction

As I sit here with my littlest one cuddled up next to me, my arm turning numb because I don't want to move and disturb his sweet slumber, I reflect on where we began long ago and where we are today. Our experience with each child and family who has entered our lives through foster care has been both formidable and sobering. Reliving many of them over again warms my heart, and the memories are such wonderful gifts. But interestingly, I have learned even more from each story after writing them out. I struggled with how much I should share of their stories; I changed their names and did not share identifiable information because these stories are deeply personal. The details are painful and beautiful, and they continue to be written every day. But I believe that if we fail to share our stories and experiences, something crucial gets lost, and each of these stories is filled with too much loss already. Their stories opened our eyes and taught us more than any other life experience ever could. I want these stories of struggle and love to mean something. I want these stories to make an impact and bring some good to you and your family the way they have for us. I want these stories to be an educational resource to shine a light on what it is to engage in foster care. In addition, all proceeds that come from this book will go directly back to OneHope27 and our mission to bring hope to kids and families involved in foster care.

I set out to describe the journey as foster care parents that opened our eyes and our hearts and changed the way we live our life. I wrote this narrative because my family has learned too much through this process to keep it to ourselves. I shudder to think of who I would be without my experience with foster care, of who my children would be. Great beauty and a God-planned passion were buried deep inside the core of our being, just waiting to be uncovered. Foster care has changed us; it's marked with sadness at times, but it has overwhelmingly opened our eyes to love and grace, and inspired us to give the same to others.

I ask that you try to be open-minded as you read about our journey, and perhaps with forgiveness for the moments when we might have made mistakes. Please know that I don't presume to believe we have it all figured out, even now. But learning and loving are a lifelong journey that we are committed to. As long as our eyes are opened to those around us, as long as we *see,* we can also engage.

According to Dictionary.com, "to foster" is "to encourage or promote the development of (something, typically something regarded as good)." As you read our story, you'll find that we did not so much "foster" as *we* were fostered. Something very good was developed in us through this process.

My husband Kevin and I love to talk about our experiences with foster care and support others in their journey. I pray that you might learn how to see those who hurt differently than you do now, that you will be filled with compassion, and perhaps that you will even be inspired to walk in these amazing shoes. If you would like further information about engaging in the foster care process, I would love to help connect you with resources in your area. You can reach me at charonne@onehope27.org.

"Compassion asks us to go where it hurts, to enter into the places of pain, to share in brokenness, fear, confusion, and anguish. Compassion challenges us to cry out with those in misery, to mourn with those who are lonely, to weep with those in tears. Compassion requires us to be weak with the weak, vulnerable with the vulnerable, and powerless with the powerless. Compassion means full immersion in the condition of being human."

Henri Nouwen

The Process

"When you know better, you do better."

Maya Angelou

Before diving into things we have learned, we have to examine the process of getting there. Kevin and I always knew that we wanted to adopt—it was one of the things we connected about when we first started dating. We figured we would adopt a child later in life once our biological kids were older, and then during a time of prayer, it hit us that the time was right then.

Kevin and I felt strongly about caring for kids from our surrounding area, and we worked with some people who had just adopted through foster care, so we met with them to ask our extensive list of questions before we moved forward. We were pleasantly surprised to hear that there was no cost to adopt through foster care other than the forty-three dollars you pay for a new birth certificate. Being a young family on a minister's salary, that was a relief to us since we worried about how we would ever be able to come up with the steep fees typically associated with adoption.

Soon after, we attended an informational meeting which was the first step in the foster care licensing process. The meeting provided an overview of foster care—why the kids come into care, what the licensing process looked like, information about the children's needs, and expectations of foster parents. I know that they explained that the goal of foster care was the reunification of families, but I can tell you we did not *hear* that. What we heard were the steps we needed to take to bring a child into our home who would stay forever. What I know now is that while kids in foster care do sometimes need adoptive homes, foster care is not an adoption agency. It is meant to be a safe place for a child for a little while so the family can heal and ultimately be put back together.

After that meeting, we filled out a foster parent interest survey that had extensive questions about our background and a checklist of sorts about the needs a child may come with as well as what we were willing to take on. I remember reading the list, fighting the guilt of saying no to a child with various needs. What I understand now is that you have to say no if you and your family can't take on the responsibility for any reason. It is far better to say no than to welcome a child into your home with needs you are not equipped to handle, only to see them transferred to a different home, creating further trauma for the child.

The entire foster-to-adopt licensing process took about four months. During that time we met with our licensing worker often, and she did a great job helping us think about what we could handle as a family. With two boys already, I really wanted a little girl, and since we wanted to keep our natural birth order in place, we were licensed for a girl of up to two years old of any racial background. Race did not matter one bit to us; we would love a child of any race. We were raising our kids to be "color blind." However, what we have learned since then is that "color blind" is more harmful than helpful. That when we don't see the God given differences in others, we rob ourselves of learning from their experiences and seeing the beauty in who they are. In addition, if we raise our kids of a different race to avoid seeing who they are, we ignore their identity and culture. If we are going to enter into foster care and/ or adopting children of a racial and cultural background from our own, we have a responsibility to learn about their culture and immerse them in understanding and love. This is a gift to us as much as a necessity for them.

During that four month licensing period, the whole family had to complete medical exams, get background checked and fingerprinted, and attend several pre-placement classes to prepare us for the journey ahead. We also had preparations to do around the house to stay up to code with foster care requirements. Many of these things seemed unnecessary to us, like having ALL of the outlets covered with those obnoxious plastic covers—even the ones up high and out of a child's reach. We needed smoke detectors in each room, not just outside each door. We also needed a fire escape plan posted on each level of the house, and emergency numbers posted by the phone.

The very first time our licensing worker came to our house, she did a walk through, opening every cupboard and door and pointing out things that we would need to move or change. Kevin had an old, dull sword that belonged to his Grandpa from the Korean War that we would either need to buy an expensive locking case for or remove from our home. The sword is now at my in-laws. It rubbed me the wrong way to have this stranger come into my home looking through my linen closet and kitchen drawers, but now I understand that if I was a mom whose child was removed from her care, I would want to know that everything about the home my child was staying in was completely safe.

Becoming licensed foster parents already felt intrusive, but perhaps even more intrusive was the one-on-one personal questioning. Our licensing worker met with our kids (who were still too little to understand what was happening or answer many of her questions), Kevin and I together, and separately as well. We were asked to share the story of our childhoods and formative years as well as give a snapshot of what our marriage was like. It was uncomfortable to say the least, even somewhat infuriating to be expected to answer such personal questions from a perfect stranger. But there is a reason for this deep dive into your personal story and history. It is to ensure that any child placed into your home will not be triggered by your experiences, or you by thiers.

When we finally finished the licensing requirements and received that piece of paper saying we were licensed foster parents able to take placement of a little girl up to two years old, we felt like the hard part was over. However, the hardest part of the journey had not even begun. Kevin, the boys, and I were just entering the unknown of foster care—the inability to predict or plan. This would be the start of an eye opening we never saw coming.

Joy

"Love recognizes no barriers. It jumps hurdles, leaps fences, and penetrates walls to arrive at its destination full of hope."

Maya Angelou

To show you where we are today and what we have learned, I have to explain to you where the journey began. Neither Kevin nor I understood much about the foster care world. We were, in all honesty, ignorant of a system full of hurting kids and families. Kevin grew up in the city, and I spent most of my formative years living in the suburbs. Regrettably, neither of our experiences growing up introduced us to the reality of the foster care system.

Our first glimpse of kids in care came when we served at a summer camp for foster children that left a permanent mark on our hearts. Kevin counseled at the weeklong camp, and I, with a newborn baby at home, helped with registration. I remember handing out new pillows to the kids as they arrived for camp, awestruck because they were given a new pillow and pillowcase—something I had taken for granted. Pillows are a given, aren't they? This realization about how so many kids don't even have the basic necessities in life—pillows, toothbrushes, plates, blankets—sparked a flame in us. We wanted to do so much more to help them, and to provide them with hope for the future. We wanted them to know that someone cared for them. It wasn't long before Kevin and I became foster parents, even though we had only been married for a few years, and we had two young children. We were also serving in *Kids and Youth Ministry* at that time, doing what we loved—impacting the lives of kids—at a church that was like home to us.

In the spring, we began the process with an informational meeting that provided an overview of foster care, the kids, and the families involved. Before we knew it, we were assigned a licensing worker to get to know our family and conduct a home study. At the end of the 120 day licensing period, we were handed a general foster license with the intention to adopt.

We only understood a little bit about the reality of foster care, and somewhat selfishly thought more about growing our family than giving a family to a child. We were licensed as adoptive resources for a girl under two years old. Kevin and I naively believed we would get a call very quickly, feeling as though our family was a great candidate with a lot of love to offer. It's a strange thing waiting for a placement call because so many emotions flooded through us. The lack of a call means there are enough homes for the kids entering care, which is wonderful because the kids have somewhere to go. Or maybe, just maybe, the children don't need to be removed from their homes at all, which is also a relief. Yet we were still anxious for the phone to ring for that child who would need us. I figured we would, at the very least, get a call for a child that did not fit our "criteria," such as a ten-year-old boy or twins, and we would have to make the difficult decision to either welcome them into our home or turn them away. The summer ended, and Thanksgiving came and went without a single phone call. Waiting somewhat impatiently, we said, "For sure, by Christmas, we will have a little baby girl to spoil and introduce to our family members as we gather together for the holidays." When Christmas passed without a call, we felt defeated, and we began to wonder if we had really heard from God. Maybe we hadn't. How could we have gotten this so wrong? It sure seemed like giving a child a stable, loving home was a good idea and the right thing to do.

Unbeknownst to us, there was a baby girl out there who would, several months later, need to be placed in a safe home. A little girl who would need a second chance at family—a family like us who might not have been available to say yes to her if they had already taken a child in.

Now, as a momma to foster children, I have had to process and come to terms with this, but I do not believe that removing children from their biological family is God's original plan for any child. I do, however, believe that God, in his restorative love, knew what Joy would need. He also knew what we would need and, in the end, I am confident that what we have learned from Joy is far greater than what we have given to her.

Spring had just begun in Wisconsin with the last snow flurry and the morning birds chirping outside of my bedroom window. After a long Wisconsin winter, spring is refreshing and rejuvenating, and it fills me with a new sense of hope. My family was busy enjoying the outdoors again, and we began going about our lives without constantly expecting the phone to ring, but our hearts still pounded when it did. And then, it happened! The call came, and I had to will myself to breathe and calm my heart which was beating out of my chest. It was an adrenaline rush, a high I had never experienced before. The voice on the other end of the phone said there was a tiny baby girl who was just removed from her home, and she needed a safe place to stay. The foster care representative led us to believe that this would be an "easy case" that would quickly progress towards adoption. We were told her name, her age, that she weighed less than nine pounds—nearly the size of our Big Boys at birth. The placement worker then said that we had just ten minutes to decide if we would open our home to this sweet, innocent little child.

After a quick and frantic phone call to Kevin, we decided, with shaking voices and trembling hands, that yes, of course we would provide a safe place for this baby girl. It was a busy Wednesday night, and we had church services and activities we were supposed to oversee, so Kevin called in emergency reinforcements who allowed me to stay home and wait for the baby to arrive. One hour later, a social worker was at our door. In her arms was a baby wrapped in blankets looking more like a newborn than an infant. At first sight, we were complete goners! We freely gave this child all of our hearts and claimed her as our own from the moment she entered our home, failing to acknowledge that she was not ours—she had a mom, she had a family who loved her and wanted her. Claiming her as ours from the start caused us to ride the ups and downs of an imperfect system much harder than we should have, making it more difficult on us as the reality of the situation presented itself.

Joy shrieked for the entire thirty minutes that the social worker was in our home. We signed papers, asked a million and one questions like, "Can we give her Tylenol? Do you know what kind of baby shampoo her mom uses? Is her skin sensitive to any lotions? Is there a bedtime routine or song she is used to hearing?" The woman sitting at our table had no answers for us. We were only given instructions about upcoming doctor appointments and given a stack of pamphlets about foster care resources. The worker also gave us a brief history about Joy that didn't even register with us because of our excitement and because of Joy's wail. What we know now is that although this was a wonderful time for us, welcoming a new child who we had so long waited for into our home, for Joy and for every other child placed in foster care it is quite possibly the worst day of their lives. Something so scary had happened to this child, and she was no longer safe to stay in her own home with her family, her bed, her toys, and everything she had ever known. I didn't smell like the mom she knew, my voice didn't register as one she had heard before, and there were all of these unfamiliar faces and sounds around her. Joy was stripped of everything she had known during her short life—good or bad—

and placed in the home of complete strangers.

That night was the longest night of our lives. We pulled out the bassinet to keep next to our bed knowing that this sweet baby needed extra closeness and comfort. I bathed her in a warm lavender bath, made sure she was fed, and put her in a blanket-soft sleeper, taking extra care to swaddle her tightly. She didn't sleep at all that night—not one little bit. None of the comfort measures I used were working. I could not soothe her, and I had never before heard screams like that. Was she horribly sick and we didn't realize it? Had we given her the wrong kind of formula, was she allergic to the lotion I put on her body, or was it just me? I had never met a baby up until this point who I could not comfort. It was the first time of many that I felt in over my head and asked myself, "What in the world have we gotten ourselves into?"

Our boys came down for breakfast concerned after hearing the night-long screaming. What was wrong with Joy? I didn't know the answer to the same question I was asking myself. All I could tell them was that I didn't know, but she had been through a lot and needed some extra love. They hugged her while she was still in my arms and asked to help give her a bottle. This was my first glimpse of the positive impact of foster care on my biological children. Here was this baby who had just entered our home who they were expected to share everything with—including their parents. A baby who kept us up all night with her siren scream and they weren't upset. They wanted to help her, to serve her, and to show her love. I was exhausted, but extremely proud of my boys, and my heart, in that moment, was full.

The next several days were a blur of our friends and family— our "village"— providing us with meals, supplies, and clothes for Joy. You see, so often children enter foster care with only the clothes on their back, and we, of course, had nothing but boys' clothing, so the pink and ruffles were all a very welcome sight. There were the caseworkers coming for the one-week check up, the mandatory doctor appointments, and our first court date. It was far more activity than I anticipated in the first week. In spite of the wonderful pre-placement classes we took in the licensing process and the months we had to mentally and emotionally prepare for the child who would come to us, I felt tremendously ill-prepared. I was a seasoned mom by this point, but I felt like a first-time momma all over again. I questioned everything and constantly felt fearful that I was doing something wrong. I can only imagine what our case manager must have thought of our ignorance and constant insecure questioning. Still, if she was bothered by our questions, she never showed it. She gracefully answered each question in a timely manner and showed us that she, too, cared about this precious child. Our case manager showed us that she cared about us, about Joy's family, and she showed us that this was not just a job for her, it was a way a life, and she gave her heart and her time for so many others.

Fear. There was so much fear in the days and months that followed. We were filled with fear at every visit Joy had with her mom, fearful about her being safe and feeling secure. Every court date we attended we feared would be the last, and a judge would say right then and there, "Joy will be going home with her 'real mom' TODAY." We feared not meeting Joy's needs well enough, not connecting appropriately with Joy's parents, or simply failing in this new role as foster parents. This was our newness into an extremely complex system that God never intended for anyone to have to walk through, not the child removed from their home, not the parents who were unable to keep their family intact, not even the foster parents, no matter their good intentions for picking up the torch. As much as we loved and adored Joy and wanted her to stay with our family forever, this whole situation we found ourselves in was an extremely complex result of a broken world that we found difficult to navigate.

I remember having lunch with our pastor's wife when we began the process of becoming foster parents. She and our pastor had two beautiful daughters who they adopted through foster care, and I wanted to share the news about Joy as well as draw wisdom from her experience. She made a statement that day from which I walked away doubting. She said, "Foster care will be the most difficult faith journey you will walk through." Thinking about all I had experienced in my childhood and early adult years including recent challenges that nearly did us in, I simply could not believe that foster care would shake my faith any further than it already had. Yet somehow we got to this place in which we were walking in complete, debilitating, all-consuming fear. Pushing that fear to the backburner and keeping our eyes on a God who loved us and loved this little girl more than we could ever fathom was a daily struggle. As it turns out, my pastor's wife was right; this was the most difficult faith journey we would walk through, but it also became the journey that built our faith, opened our eyes, and taught us more about the love of our God than anything we had experienced before.

Joy had three visits with her mom every week and sometimes additional visits with dad. Sending my baby off in a car with a visitation worker I didn't know was gut wrenching, every single time. Her visits were supervised in a cold, institutional visitation center, which was really just an office building of individual rooms with a used sofa and a pile of toys for the kids. There was a worker in eye and earshot at all times to keep Joy safe, but I feared that we had very different ideas of what "safe" was. Between driving time and the court mandated visitation hours, Joy would end up gone for half the day and come back an emotional mess every time. Kevin and I spent hours holding and comforting her when she returned from visits, repeating the mantra, "You are home and you are safe." It was emotionally and mentally exhausting for all of us.

As Joy grew into toddlerhood she began to verbalize that she didn't want to go on visits. She would cling to me and plead with her big brown eyes for me to protect her, keep her safe, and not make her go as the visitation worker would literally peel her away from my arms. Visitation is important in foster care because the main goal of this system is to see a biological family whole, healthy, and reunited, so a continued bond between parents and children is vital. I wholeheartedly believe in healing, and I believe in second chances. I believe that children belong with their families they are born into when at all possible, but I also believe in looking out for the best interest of the children. A child's right to grow up healthy, whole, and safe should not be overshadowed by the rights of a parent. For Joy, visitation was traumatizing. We saw it first hand, and the workers saw it first hand, but we would never receive court permission to cease visits. We would not understand just how deeply traumatizing this time was until much later when the help of a skilled therapist made sense of it all.

Communication with Joy's parents was difficult to bridge. We sent notebooks and pictures along with her on visits to share how she was spending her days in our home and to share milestones or doctor's instructions. I was somewhat uncomfortable sharing the details of our life without seeming pompous, bragging about what we had, or how well she was doing. Yet I wanted a confirmation

from her mother—the first, most important person in Joy's life—
that she recognized how much we cared for her daughter, that she
saw how we loved Joy, and that it mattered.

I am not someone who looks back with regret, wanting to
change aspects of my life. I wholeheartedly believe that we learn
from the mistakes we made. I believe that the positive and negative
things we go through make us who we are. But if I were ever to have
the opportunity to change something in my past, it would be the
way I felt toward and interacted with Joy's parents. I would spend
more time getting to know them and learning about their family
make up and traditions. I would spend more time opening my heart,
relinquishing judgment and bias that I didn't even know I harbored.

It pains me, but is imperative to admit today the negative
attitude we had toward Joy's parents. We, at this time, bought into
the lie that our children's parents were the enemy. It breaks my
heart to think of the relationship we might have had, the support
we might have provided, the good we might have done if our eyes
had been opened to them. Her mother had been hardened by her
involvement with social services, and I did nothing to help change
her view. Sadly, it would be years before we learned to walk in love
with the parents of children who were placed in our home.

Days and months passed much the same way for the next
couple of years. There would be a few nice days with Joy in between
visits when she would relax, let her guard down, and just play like
a typical toddler would—until mid-week when visits started all
over again, and this dance of soothing and comforting and doing
absolutely everything we could to show this little girl that she was
safe and we could be trusted. Joy never relaxed in our arms or
reciprocated affection, she did not look us in the eye, she struggled
with peer interactions, she screamed all of the time at octaves so

high I was surprised the windows in our home weren't shattered. She needed rigidity with routines and expectations, and she was still very tiny, barely one percent on the growth chart. Joy needed a great deal of warning if her routine was about to be adjusted. If I changed our plans, if I walked up and kissed her without warning or did something even the slightest bit differently than I had done it the time before, it would send Joy into hour-long, uncontrollable meltdowns that were terrifying to watch. Even at that young age, Joy fought for control at every turn. By the middle of her second year of life, it was clear that something was happening with Joy that was beyond our parenting abilities, and we needed professional advice.

We scheduled an evaluation with a children's therapist who came highly recommended. After a few sessions with her, she diagnosed Joy with Autism Spectrum Disorder. I was blindsided as she shared her findings with me, and I was in utter shock by this diagnosis. I had some experience with kids on the spectrum, and Joy did not seem to struggle the same way any of them did. However, the majority of the children I knew with ASD were boys, and girls often presented differently, so perhaps this was the answer we were looking for and provided the direction we needed to take in order to help our little girl. We tried to come to terms with this doctor's findings; how was it fair that this sweet little girl, who had already been through so much, would also have to struggle for the rest of her life with Autism? As we dealt with this diagnosis with fear and uncertainty about Joy's future, we dove into therapy in an attempt to develop the tools she would need to succeed. I prayed often during this time that if this diagnosis would impact Joy's life and future that it would not be wasted, and God would make good of it.

While Joy was in therapy, I spent much of my time reading and researching how to parent a child on the Autism spectrum and how to help her thrive. Between my research and her lack of response to the hours of therapy she was engaged in, I began to question this diagnosis once again. I was familiar with what trauma was. However, I had very little knowledge of or training about its effects on a child.

I ordered every book that I could find on the topic, I joined support groups, and I scoured the Internet for blog posts and research. It became increasingly apparent that our Joy was suffering from the effects of trauma, not Autism. I was a motivated momma on the hunt to help my precious girl; however, there were not many professionals well-versed in trauma in our area. After months of searching, we finally found a psychologist who had experience with both Autism and trauma to help us sort out the diagnoses. Several sessions and an in-depth evaluation later, she confirmed our suspicions that, while a child who has been traumatized could appear to have some Autism-like tendencies, what our child was struggling with was, in fact, the effects of trauma both in utero and in her early life.

Our new therapist explained to us that Joy was in a constant state of fight, flight, or freeze, and that her body's level of alertness was always heightened. When most people sit at a baseline of thirty percent anxiety, she was sitting at sixty to seventy percent, so the littlest thing could push her over the edge. The therapy we had her in was actually doing more harm than good because she was gone from us, her "safe people," too much, and her healing needed to come through connection. As a master of trauma-informed care, Dr. Karyn Purvis writes in *The Connected Child,* "[These] children were harmed in relationships, and they will experience healing through nurturing relationships." We were heartbroken as we began to understand what our little girl had been through.

We wanted to be able to take it from her, to change what she had experienced. However, knowing that was not in our power, we resolved to become part of her healing.

We were going through a challenging court process at that time that would decide where Joy would continue to grow up. The trial was devastating beyond anything I have ever experienced. As I took the stand to answer questions about how Joy handled visits with her parents, about who she calls 'momma,' about what comforts her and what scares her, I remember sharing a story about the night before when Joy was scared and had a difficult time going to sleep. I found her in her six-year-old brother's room looking to him for comfort and security. He had his arm around her and was reading one of the books he was just learning to read to her. After putting Joy back to bed in her own room with extra cuddles and assurance, I peeked back in my son's room to find a bed set up on his floor which he told me was for Joy in case she got scared and needed him again. Telling this story to the judge, my voice began to crack, and tears started to well up in my eyes both at the realization that we had become Joy's home and that this day would dictate whether or not she would remain with us or return to her parents.

A man I had never met before took the stand after me. He resembled Joy's father, but carried himself with pride and poise. As he began answering the attorney's questions, I learned that he didn't just resemble his son, Joy's father, but they also shared a name. James and his son also shared a similar story of hardship that lead to time spent in foster care themselves; however, their response to the challenges that life threw at them could not have been more different. The James on the stand that day faced the adversities in his life and grew stronger because of them. I listened attentively, and it became clear that the defense was vying for James to take guardianship of Joy rather than us adopting her. My heart dropped, turned, and flipped, and I had to will myself to continue breathing steadily. James had, unbeknownst to me, been attending visits with Joy for several weeks previous to the trial. James spoke of his desire to keep Joy with family and his own negative experience growing up in foster care. As he spoke, our incomparable Assistant District Attorney looked over at me reassuringly as if to say, "She's not going anywhere, Joy is going home with you today," yet I sat there, terrified that a blood relative would win custody, and we would go home with empty hands and shattered hearts.

To our relief, the judge assigned to our case saw what was in the best interest for our girl. I will never forget the feeling of hearing him say that although James was blood, WE were who Joy knew, we were her family, and it was in her best interest to continue to grow up with us.

After a long day of testimonies and intense emotions, the verdict was in, and I could hardly settle my breath or control the water works, especially after looking over at Joy's mom, a mom who was losing her child. You see, we "won" that day. Our daughter got to stay in our home, and it was declared that she would forever be a part of our family. But Joy's mother lost everything that day, and there was a deep loss for Joy, too. No child should have to lose their parents. I was in no way prepared for the extremely diverse emotions that I would feel—everything from complete brokenness to utter elation.

Her parents lost Joy that day, and in the days that followed I nearly did as well. I nearly lost sight of Joy in trying to "fix" her. I desperately wanted my love for my daughter to be enough to make her pain disappear. I truly thought if I loved her well enough it would be all she needed, and "All you need is love," right? I found myself blaming others for the pain and suffering that our daughter carried with her, I found myself questioning why God would allow her to be born into this situation, why He, in His omniscience, didn't pluck this beautiful, innocent child out of the pain she had experienced. It wasn't fair that Joy was living with the effects of what was done to her and what wasn't done for her in her early life. It wasn't fair that I now had to try and pick up the pieces and carry her into healing. It was not my most graceful time; it was by all accounts pretty ugly. This was an isolating period for me. I hid these very real feelings from those around me because I didn't want to give adoption, or quite honestly myself, a bad rap. In my heart I still knew great beauty could come out of this brokenness, and I was incredibly aware that the world around me was watching for it, too.

Reaching the end of my rope, I let go of my anger, and more than anything, a fear of inadequacy that I would never be enough for Joy. I hunkered down, delved further into trauma awareness, and learned how to love my child the way she needed me to, not simply out of my own expectations for her. To be a "trauma momma" is to be a "special needs momma" and all that comes with it—good and bad. The greatest thing I have realized as a special needs momma is to rejoice over the little things—the things that seem like normal, everyday occurrences, but for Joy, they are not. It's the time she came home from school telling me she made a new friend; the time she came to me telling me she was hurt and looking for my comfort instead of retreating into herself; it's the time she got invited to join the competitive gymnastics team when we only joined for therapeutic reasons; it's the time she left a note on the fridge that said, "I Love Familee," when you know the concept of family is deeply complex for her; and it's the time she calmly came to me and said, "Momma, I'm scared. Will you lie down with me for a little while?" I treasure all of these things and tuck them deep away in my heart to remember in the more challenging moments.

As for James Sr., we saw his love for his granddaughter when he spoke on the stand that day, and we heard enough of his story to believe she would be safe with him. Over the years, he became a part of our family. James expressed many times that Joy ended up right where she needed to be, and that we were exactly the family she needed. Even more, he said that we changed his view of foster care. We are incredibly thankful for this man, who has become "Papa J" to all of us. And we likely would not have known him if it wasn't for his fight for her in court. He is, at this time, the only biological family member Joy has contact with because of her trauma-related anxiety disorder. He is safe, and he doesn't trigger Joy's anxiety. I send pictures to her mom and stay in touch with her. It's my hope that when Joy has the tools to handle interacting with her mom, that mom will also be in a healthy place for us to make that happen.

I am Joy's momma. I put her to sleep at night, care for her when she is hurt or sick, and I share history and memories with her that are special to us. Still, I know she has history with another mom who is special only to them, but that doesn't diminish my role in her life as much as mine doesn't diminish hers. Walking through this lifelong journey of adoption is messy and complicated, but I would walk through it all over again for Joy.

This child, my daughter, has completely stolen my heart. My heart aches for her in a way I have never known before. I would do anything to protect her and keep her from experiencing any more heartbreak in life, but I know I can't fully protect her from life's lessons. Sometimes I look at her in awe of the strength and resilience she exhibits in her tiny frame. I have learned that love is not the absence of heartbreak, and that sometimes the two coexist in a beautifully painful dance. Joy has come to understand that she is loved unconditionally which, when all is said and done, is everything we want her to know. Joy is deeply and completely loved. Joy is loved by a Heavenly Father who is her Creator. He takes great delight in her and will never leave her. She's loved by a first mom and a first dad who wanted her and chose to give her life. She is loved by some amazing big brothers who would do anything to protect her. She is loved by little brothers who look up to her and feel safe and secure with her. She is loved by a large network of extended friends and family, and Joy is loved by a momma and dadda who will never give up on her, and will spend their lives showing her that she is wanted, she is precious, she is strong, she is cherished, and she is safe.

> *17 "For the Lord your God is living among you.*
> *He is a mighty savior.*
> *He will take delight in you with gladness.*
> *With his love, he will calm all your fears.*
> *He will rejoice over you with joyful songs."*
>
> *Zephaniah 3:17*

Ivy

"We're hardwired for connection."

Brene Brown

Ivy is a beautiful girl, tall with a perfect natural wave to her hair and a smile that easily hides the hardship of her life. When Ivy smiles, it looks genuine, and if you didn't know any better you would believe that it was. However, I know Ivy's story. I know that she grew up in foster care, dealing with how her mom abandoned her—the one person who should have always been there for her. And as a result, Ivy battles that deep-rooted abandonment in every aspect of her life. Ivy has trouble moving on from it, and doesn't consider herself worthy.

Ivy did not graduate high school, she is homeless, jobless, and fighting to get control of her mental and emotional health. She wants to better herself, but she doesn't know if better exists. What Ivy wants more than anything is to know, without a doubt, that she is loved by someone—by anyone.

Sadly, Ivy's story is not a stand alone case. I have seen a little bit of Ivy in every child and parent we have met through foster care. There is a cycle that develops, and it must be broken somewhere along the line. For too many families, the destructive cycle of neglect and families being broken apart transfers from generation to generation.

I am not certain what the answer is to this multifaceted problem. What I know for sure is that making an impact on kids and families in foster care will take a sincere desire to be close to others. It will take us crossing the street to meet our neighbor, a single mom with a brood of children who looks overwhelmed to the point of tears every time you park the car and wave to her in passing. Bring her some cookies and coffee (we all know she could use that coffee), and sit without an agenda other than to begin a conversation and get to know her. There is no need to share anything other than your love—the only real agent of change. It may be that you change the life of that mom and her kids or the dad you see at school drop off every morning but never took the time to get to know, but it will certainly change you and open your eyes, and when our eyes are opened and our hearts engaged we can make a difference in the lives of those around us.

I wish that someone had engaged with Ivy's mom in this way. Imagine if a neighbor had crossed the street and gotten to know and love *her* family. Perhaps that neighbor would have made a positive impact, and her family's experience would have been different. Or maybe this neighbor's home would have been a safe place for the kids to go to when the worst happened. Certainly a neighbor taking the time to get to know the family across the street might have shown Ivy that she is not alone, and she is worthy of love.

Bubba and My Hero

*"Brothers are like streetlights along the road,
they don't make distance any shorter, but they
light up the path and make the walk worthwhile."*

Author Unknown

It was a beautiful summer day, the sun was shining bright, there was the slightest breeze, and it was just warm enough to feel hope for the gorgeous days to come after a season full of dreariness and rain. I packed up Joy and our other foster daughter and headed to the park—the day was just too perfect to stay indoors. While digging in the sand and building castles together, I received a call from social services about a little boy named Bubba.

For weeks leading up to this call I had agonized over this very moment. When we learned that Joy's mom was pregnant again, I wanted to tell the social worker that yes, we would take the baby if he was removed from his mom's care and needed a safe place to stay, but I worried about how Joy would handle it. There is no manual for this kind of thing, no chapter in the elusive "great book of parenting" that instructs you how to open your home to your adopted child's sibling. Trying to determine if this was the best thing for Joy or if it would completely crush her consumed my thoughts. What if her mom got it together enough that Bubba could return home—how would Joy handle that? How could I bring Joy's brother to us, knowing that we might have to send him away? I spent hours, days, weeks really praying and begging God to speak to me and tell me what to do. He didn't instruct me with an audible voice or flash of lightning, but He did send me a friend who had already had to make a similarly tough decision.

I have always considered my friend, Ann, a foster parent all-star. She walked this road several years before us and had done so with grace and faith. Not long ago, Ann and her family welcomed in her adopted daughter's brother. After spending quite some time in their home as a member of the family, the little brother did return home to his mom. As Ann shared her story with me, her powerful words shaped a new perspective for me and have stayed with me ever since. She said, "I will never regret giving my daughter the chance to know her brother." In spite of the pain in watching him go, in not being able to raise brother and sister together, they knew each other when they otherwise might not have, and it made it all worth it.

Ann was more right than I could ever had imagined. From the moment we took Bubba home, he and Joy shared a bond that is impossible to describe. Joy was connected with her big brothers, our biological sons, but her relationship with her little brother was profoundly deep. This bond was a gift to the two of them, and quite honestly to our entire family—watching them bond was a constant visual reminder of hope, of harmony, and of love.

Bubba came to us right after he was born. On the day that our kids' mom went into preterm labor, she called to inform me that her water had broken earlier than expected, and she was at the hospital, so it wouldn't be long. She said that she had called to let me know that she would miss her visit with Joy tomorrow, but in my gut I knew there was more to her story. I asked if anyone was there with her, and she assured me that her best friend was on her way. We made plans to bring Joy to meet her new baby brother the following day, then I hung up the phone with a knot in my stomach.

The following morning, after Joy awoke, I told her that her baby brother had been born, and we would be going to meet him soon. I called her mom to see if we could bring anything that she might need. When she answered the phone, her voice was filled with exhaustion and sadness—or was it loneliness? I wondered if something had happened to Bubba. As she spoke, she explained that her friend never showed up, that she was in a sterile hospital room by herself, with no support, no one there who loved her, no one to talk her through contractions or to hold her hand. She was alone, giving birth to a baby that she might not ever be allowed to take home.

The walls I had built around my heart to keep Joy's mom out began to crumble that day. My eyes opened a little bit more, and when Joy and I got to the hospital I saw, for the first time, a mere girl who had no support. Who felt unloved, and maybe had never truly known what love was. I truly *saw* her, and I was filled with compassion for her that I had never felt before. That day in the hospital room, with a daughter we both wanted and a newborn baby who would later come home to us, I began to love their mom. My eyes were opened to the pain she had experienced, and the more I saw her, the more I saw the pain all around me. I only thought that I'd see a little bit of hurt when I chose to become part of the foster care system, but once my eyes opened completely, I could no longer choose which kind of hurt I saw; I saw it all.

Joy is the reason we call him Bubba. Our little girl was so proud of her brother, but she couldn't quite put the syllables together, so she would introduce every friend and stranger to her "Baby Bubba." He quickly became her prize possession. If Bubba was awake, Joy was right there with him. Watching Joy step into the role of big sister was something I cherished. Knowing that Joy hadn't been nurtured early in her life, I wondered if she would bond with him. I was amazed to see how quickly she connected with her baby brother. Joy soothed him, and she wanted to help feed him and assist with his diaper changes. Even at a young age, Joy's nurturing nature was remarkable.

This little preemie, Bubba Boy, quickly grew into a sweet, round bundle of fun. He had the most adorable pudgy face, chubby-stubby legs, and an easy going spirit. Bubba was simply a breath of fresh air. He had a couple of medical issues to work through, and they required appointments with specialists and physical therapy. Even through the appointments and the tests, he was happy and content, and he quickly stole the heart of every doctor and therapist, just as he had stolen ours. To this day, Bubba is a sweetheart of a boy, making sure that he gives his momma a hug and a kiss every day. In the afternoon, he will say, "Oh! I didn't give you a hug and kiss yet today." I gladly accept it without reminding him that he did in fact give me a hug and kiss just a few minutes earlier. Bubba loves everything his big brothers love. He cheers for their favorite sports teams and imitates his brothers' victory dances. He is a daddy's boy, asking multiple times throughout the day when Dadda will be home from work, but he still loves me wholeheartedly, and he invents games we can play together. I cherish these sweet memories, all the while knowing there is another momma out there who isn't able to have these priceless moments with him. The reminder is sobering.

Bubba had visits with Joy and their mom for a short time. Visits were not as difficult for Bubba as they were for Joy; we have his gentle temperament to thank for that. We also have Joy to thank who, knowing visits could be hard, would pack special toys and blankets for Bubba and was the first one to comfort him when he would cry during those visitations.

Less than two years after he entered our lives, we adopted Bubba. No one was more excited that day than his sister. Joy proudly wore the dress from her own adoption day and bounced from wall to wall with contagious excitement. This was our second adoption, and it was no less special than the first. After the trauma our kids had experienced, after the pain of losing the mother who they had bonded with as they formed within her, there was finally beauty in the situation. Bubba and Joy, brother and sister, would grow up together just as siblings should, and they would be a part of our family forever. We felt complete. Until we unexpectedly received a call about another baby brother, and the voice on the other end of the line asked if we would open our home to him as well. My eyes welled up, and I could not hold back the tears that drenched my sleeve as I wiped them away right there in the middle of a Target diaper isle.

My immediate thoughts were of a mom who was, at that very moment, saying goodbye to a child, her newborn baby. Then my thoughts went to me, at home, my husband out of town, and five kids under the age of eleven. Did I have the strength and energy to be up all night by myself with a baby and give the other four what they needed during the day? It wasn't the first time I felt overwhelmed as a foster parent, and it wasn't the first time I questioned my ability to do it, but something about this time was different, and I struggled to pull myself together.

Kevin is my teammate, my steadfast rock, and my comic relief. He is strong in every area I am weak, and he is exactly the partner God knew I needed. Kevin was already on the road to a funeral of a close friend's father. I couldn't ask him to turn around, I couldn't ask him to come home just because I needed him—his friend needed him, too. It was an impossible situation with no easy solution. So, by necessity, I chose to practice giving. Giving my husband to a friend who needed his support, giving my fear about handling everything to God, and giving my home to the baby who needed us.

The baby came later that day in the arms of the umpteenth

social worker to walk through our door. Our older boys were still at school when the baby arrived, so imagine their surprise when they got off the bus and opened the door to me holding a "born baby" as Joy would say. To my delight, just like all of the other times before, they responded with excitement and eagerness to dive right in and help. I recall one of my boys saying, "Wait until my teacher hears about this!" and the other said that he was looking forward to telling his friends about the new baby. Foster care has no doubt made these boys who they are today. There is no better way to teach your kids to give and love and serve others than by inviting another child into their home who they have to share everything with, including their parents.

One by one the kids took turns holding the baby, checking out his little fingers, tiny toes, and gushing over how cute and small he was. Joy's turn came, and as she held him, she comforted him and began referring to him as "My Hero." I still don't know where this term came from, but it was the most precious thought to me, that a little girl could see her newborn baby brother as her hero. It was one of those moments when you wonder if a child's simple understanding of the world exceeds yours. It was as if she instinctively knew what he had gone through, and she understood the inner strength he would need to thrive. She saw this in him and celebrated it. This time around we not only had the pleasure of watching Joy and one brother's bond, but also the satisfaction of watching the three of them connect as one little unit. I worried, as all moms do, that adding a new baby to the family would create jealousy, but there was none of that. Bubba loved his little brother, fiercely, from the start. I have pictures upon pictures of those first days when Bubba climbed into the bouncy seat with My Hero or laid next to him during tummy time. My favorite picture, which is forever imprinted in my heart, is one of both of the little guys in the bouncy seat—Bubba with his arm around My Hero, kissing him on the cheek, big brother and little brother together.

We made it through that weekend with Kevin away. I exhaled in deep relief when he pulled in the driveway, and I ran into his arms, crying the last few tears I had left. The kids couldn't wait to introduce him to the baby. I chuckled as they attempted to surprise him with My Hero as if Kevin didn't know, as if we hadn't spoken about this new baby while he was away. That night we ate a picnic dinner in the living room, watched a movie, and took turns cuddling My Hero in our first moments together as a family of seven.

By the time My Hero came to us, we had adopted Joy, fostered several other children, one of whom is Bubba, and we would be adopting him soon. In addition, we had provided respite care (longer term babysitting for foster parents) for several other children. In welcoming My Hero, bringing our household number up to seven, some people began to question our sanity and why we would open our home and our hearts to another child. We even had a few individuals who asked, "Haven't you done enough already?" as if there was a limit to what was expected of us as foster care parents that we had unknowingly surpassed. To the outside world looking in, we were crazy to say yes again, and maybe we were. I've learned that to engage in something meaningful, something life changing, there needs to be an element of crazy in all of us. This journey has become a passion, one that we have thrown ourselves into headfirst, and we don't regret it one bit.

My Hero didn't sleep through the night until he was over two years old; he just never wanted to slow down! He was always right in the center of the action, and he never wanted to miss a moment of fun. He has a contagious belly laugh that jiggles his entire body, and he is constantly imitating his favorite race car, Lightning McQueen.

My Hero and Bubba are now the best of friends. They share a room, share toys, and even share clothes although they are nearly two years apart in age. When one brother is not there, the other constantly asks when his brother will be back, or he talks to him like he is still in the room. I didn't know how My Hero would handle it when his big brother went to school in the fall; he'd miss him terribly during the day, but I knew the celebration when we picked Bubba up from school would be monumental.

My Hero was, and still is, the busiest little guy I have ever met. During his first year and a half of life he wouldn't play with toys, instead opting to scour the house for things he could get into and make a mess of. He still manages to get into everything, and he can destroy a room faster than any child I've known. As My Hero got older and stronger, he seemed to become increasingly less aware of his size or age; he just figured he could do anything his older siblings could. Nothing stopped that boy, and everyday I discovered a little more of that inner strength that Joy first saw in him as a newborn. He will need to draw from this strength the more he begins to process his story. It's sobering to think of the day he starts to ask questions and he begins to put the pieces together. I am painstakingly aware that I will not have all of the answers, and I may not be able to fully understand the emotions that will impact Joy, Bubba, and My Hero. They will process the ins and outs of their journeys differently, but because they grew up together, they will have each other, and us, to lean on.

There is a snapshot that I love of our three adopted children. Joy is sitting in a swing, gently holding newborn My Hero, and Bubba has his arms wrapped around them both. I was lucky enough to capture that moment, and since then I have taken hundreds of pictures of them cuddled together in everyday activities like watching a movie, playing a game, swinging, coloring . . . but every time I reflect on the way their lives might have been. Every day I am thankful that "the littles," as we affectionately call them, are growing up together as siblings, just the way they should. We found it fitting to place this image on the backside of My Hero's adoption announcement with the phrase, "Together Forever," because that day was about more than just *our* forever with My Hero. His adoption was also about the togetherness of three *siblings*, forever.

Rebecca

*"Being deeply loved by someone gives you strength,
while loving someone deeply gives you courage."*

Lao Tzu

I first Met Rebecca at court, which would turn out to be the place we would spend the majority of our time together. Rebecca was several years younger than me, but her face looked aged after a lifetime of tragedy. She spoke like an adult, but with the attitude of a rebellious teenager who was mad at the world. She said everything that came to her mind and apologized for nothing. Rebecca was tough and cold, and just when you thought you were making headway with her, she would put up walls again. Her life experiences taught her the tragic art of shutting people out. Rebecca is one of the biological moms we've worked with, yet in many ways Rebecca is every mom we've met because of foster care.

During the first several years I knew her, I made half-hearted attempts to build a relationship with the woman who loved a child I also loved. I felt obligated to speak with her, but I didn't hope for the best. In my mind, Rebecca had made her choices, and I had to protect this child at all costs. I tried to keep in touch with Rebecca, and I was friendly when I was with her, but secretly I feared her, I resented her, and I did not understand why she said the things she did and made the choices that she made. I was angry for the way Rebecca's choices affected this child, and I didn't understand why she couldn't just do better.

One time Rebecca showed up for one of her child's doctor appointments. Naturally, I was concerned about needing to see this specialist, and naturally Rebecca was concerned—this was still her child, after all. I was glad to see her there, yet at the same time I dreaded interacting with her over the next several hours. We struggled to determine which mom would take the lead answering the doctor's questions and explaining our concerns. I imagine it wasn't particularly comfortable for the medical staff. I was the one who had been taking care of this child for months, and I fought for control as if I was clawing my way to the top of a mountain, obliterating everything in my path. If I could go back to this day we shared at the specialist's clinic, I would take the opportunity to ask Rebecca about her life, her story—her child's history. I would ask what her hopes and dreams were for her child's future. I would connect and bond with her instead of fighting her every step of the way.

Many people who see a child removed from their parents' care due to abuse or neglect immediately think the parents are the enemy. Unknowingly, that is what I did. I vilified Rebecca in my mind, and my heart became increasingly hardened toward her. I feared that Rebecca's success would mean my heartbreak if her success meant that her child could return home to her. Every time she made a mistake, we logged it as evidence of her ineptitue. When we could have supported her, we stood and watched her fall. When we could have spoken life to her, we stayed silent. When we could have shown love to her, we stood still. Although we didn't do anything hurtful or unkind, our attitude certainly didn't express love. We saw a limited picture of who Rebecca was and simply did not understand how she could let all of this happen.

When Rebecca found herself in a difficult situation *again,* I felt very little sympathy or grace. Sure, I listened to her stories as we sat outside the courtroom waiting for our case to be called, all the while judging her choices and actions. It was beyond me why she hadn't learned from her past experiences and made any changes to the life she was living. But I also didn't understand that she had been through trauma of her own and that maybe this was the best she could do.

The more I interacted with Rebecca, the more I understood her story, the more my heart broke for her. When other moms' stories and more experiences in the world of foster care opened my eyes, it opened them wide, and I began to see it all. I wanted to build a bridge to Rebecca to show her the love I had been withholding—the love the world had been withholding.

But, oh, did I have work to do. I had already spent much of my relationship with Rebecca keeping her at arm's length. If I were to genuinely love Rebecca, I would have to let go of my misconceptions. I had a great deal of trust to build with her, and I wasn't sure if she would ever put her guard down long enough to let me in. It was certainly going to take time, but time was something I figured we had. Looking back, I didn't do much differently other than when I asked Rebecca how she was, I asked with compassion and true concern. I found more opportunities to encourage her parenting and praise her for the amazing child she created. I no longer hoped she would fail; I wanted to see her succeed. I wanted her to believe that even after her mistakes and missteps and the traumatic things that she had experienced in life, she could hope for more; she could, with love and support, make things better for herself. I wanted Rebecca happy and whole for herself first and foremost, and her health would no doubt influence the well-being of her child.

Little by little, Rebecca began to open up. Sometimes she would confide in me about the details of her child protective services case, which made it apparent that she had no one else to share with. To some, this would seem unhealthy or unnatural, but to me, this was progress. Knowing that Rebecca had someone she could talk to no matter what the topic was, who would hear her and respond in love, was an important step forward. I felt honored to have earned a place in Rebecca's life. Still, I was the woman currently raising her child, and sometimes that created a barrier between us whether I wanted it to or not. It was there, and it could not be denied.

After the case closed, I was left wondering if we had succeeded in making an impact on Rebecca's life, if we had succeeded in showing her love. Though it was likely that we would never know for sure, I began to rest knowing that we found the space to do what was right when it came to Rebecca, and I could only hope that she saw that, too. Then the day came that Rebecca needed help again, and she asked for us to step in. It was at that moment when we knew we had made a difference. We had made a difference.

Amayah

"We think sometimes that poverty is only being hungry, naked, and homeless. The poverty of being unwanted, unloved, and uncared for is the greatest poverty. We must start in our own homes to remedy this kind of poverty."

Mother Teresa

As I mentioned before, we entered foster care with a naive understanding of a complex system. The more we experienced the daily struggle, the more we saw the needs of the children and the realities of the families connected to them, the more we knew what we needed to do. We began volunteering at our licensing agency, joining committees, helping with projects and events, writing blog posts . . . but still we were not satisfied; we knew we had more to give. That's when we decided to expand our license with the hope to do what we thought we could never do—emergency short-term placements. We agonized as we considered the possibility of having a new child in our home, even for a short time, and then giving him or her back; this is often the main reason why many people say that they could never be foster parents.

We received a call about a little girl who was a year older than Joy, and we were told she would be arriving at our home within the hour. I quickly tried to throw something in the crock-pot for dinner anticipating the crazy afternoon that was to come, and I ran downstairs to see what clothes we had stored away in her size. Unfortunately, there wasn't much in storage. However, there wasn't any time to shop for supplies because the doorbell rang, and our new baby was placed in our arms.

When I opened the door to meet Amayah for the first time, she instantly stretched out her arms for me to hold her, which caught me by surprise. After everything that she must have experienced that day, she didn't shy away from me at all. In fact, she was the opposite. She was so clingy that I couldn't put her down for one second or even walk across the room without her breaking down. This would become the new normal with Amayah. After the case manager relayed the typical instructions and information then curtly walked out of the door, I had a chance to look at Amayah more closely. I looked at her, and then I looked over at Joy. She didn't look like she was a year older than Joy at all. I looked at her paperwork to discover that the math was wrong. Amayah was the same age as Joy; they even shared a birthday a few weeks apart in the same month. These girls were peers, twins really.

The boys came home to find another child in their home, but it didn't faze them one bit. They tried to talk with her and welcome her in, but she would have none of it. I assured them that Amayah would just need a little time. When Kevin walked through the door, Amayah took one look at him and let loose a sound of sheer terror, and she immediately tried to scale my body, desperate for safety. Her response was more than bizarre. Never have I seen a child react to Kevin with even an inkling of fear. He was a children's pastor by trade, a big kid, a goofball, and a harmless teddy bear who children wanted to be around, not run from in fear. Often in the foster care system, you only receive pieces of the child's story. It is up to the foster family to put the puzzle pieces together to help bring healing. Amayah's behavior revealed a piece of the puzzle that we were not previously aware of.

Since I had no time to run out for supplies and clearly could not leave Amayah home with Kevin, I left the other kids home with him, and I took Amayah to the store with me. She had not spoken anything other than "mommy." She just kept repeating, "mommy, mommy, mommy." It pierced my heart every time she spoke that name, and I thought about what this beautiful child must have experienced. I also worried knowing that Amayah looked nothing like me and was constantly crying out for her mommy, that people would think I stole her, especially considering my cart was filled to the brim with a new crib mattress, diapers, car seat, and clothes. It's in moments like that when you wish you had worn your "proud foster parent" shirt that day. Thankfully, we made it through our run for supplies that night without further issue. Amayah passed out in the car on the way home, exhausted by the trauma of the day.

Amayah was a little girl who was obviously hurting on the inside. Children are not removed from their home just because of poverty; they are removed because of abuse and/or neglect. However, in this situation, poverty played a significant role. Amayah had been living in a very impoverished situation. She did not live in permanent housing, and she had very few possessions which explained why the shoes she was wearing were two sizes too small. We were told that Amayah didn't play with toys. In fact, she didn't really own toys. But once, as Joy talked on a play phone, Amayah picked up a doll and held it to her ear. She didn't know how to properly play with toys. It was a sobering and distressing experience. Playing should be natural for a child, not something that has to be taught. It that moment, I was struck with the sovereignty that brought Amayah to a home with a twin-like peer to show her how to be a child.

Caring for Amayah was exhausting; she demanded all of my attention and still barely let me walk several feet from her without breaking down. This made things especially difficult considering the three other small children in our home who also needed me. The word that was constantly on my mind in that season was "worn." I was worn thin and weary, and I was most certainly overwhelmed. All of the young children in our house needed me constantly; there was very little time to myself, and there was no way that we could leave Amayah with a babysitter yet. She just wasn't ready. I was headed straight for burnout. However, I kept going because they needed me to. Giving into the weariness was not an option.

Finances were tight as a family of six on one salary. Although we were given a stipend to help provide for the children in our care, non-fostering families often misconstrued it as a big fat paycheck. This stipend is meant to offset the care of the child, and that is truly all it does. We were not making money off of each child in the foster care system, and that was in no way our intention for providing foster care. We definitely struggled to make ends meet, but God always provided enough. We had learned long ago that He responds to our faithfulness to Him.

Amayah didn't smile for the first week with us—not a smirk, not a little turning in the corner of her mouth. Nothing. She looked so sad, and I wanted to take the sadness away from her or just carry it for a little while so she could feel what it meant to rest. One evening, while Kevin and some of the other kids were at church, I was home with one of the Big Boys and Amayah. He was trying to pull Amayah out of her shell a little bit and began playing a game of peekaboo with her. It truly touched my heart. Before I knew it, Amayah released her death grip on me and began chasing my Big Boy around the house, laughing, and that's when we saw it for the first time—her smile. A smile so bright that it filled her face and lit up the entire room. Her cherubic smile glowed long enough for me to take a mental picture of this moment—a picture that is a treasured memory of, hands down, my favorite moment in foster care. Not only were we gifted with seeing a darling smile for the first time, but also it was our son who brought it out of her. This moment was a gift that we would hold tightly to during rough days to come.

We began to build a relationship with Amayah's mom, Jashanna. From the start, it was very different from the relationships we had with other moms of the kids who came to us. She was respectful, appreciative, and open with us. She did not view us as the enemy, and we had learned enough about her to view her as one. I would often meet Jashanna on a non-visit day somewhere fun so she could have more time with her daughter. I remember the first time Jashanna referred to me as Amayah's "other mommy," a moment that rocked my heart with both deep sadness and deep appreciation. It is an incredible gift to be granted the permission to care for another mother's child as your own. Jashanna had been living in poverty and had very little support in her life; I was convinced that's what she had been missing. I believed that with our help and support, she could parent Amayah safely, and her family could be put back together. Jashanna started following her court ordered terms for reunification and began to dream of her future, making plans accordingly. Kevin and I began to dream of being a beautiful part of a family reunification. We dreamed about the day we would no longer be foster mom and dad, and instead serve in an aunt and uncle role, believing we would always be a part of this family's life. We were not just fostering Amayah; we were fostering hope and healing in Jashanna as well. This co-parenting, supportive relationship is the best-case scenario in foster care.

The hair! Up until this point I didn't know anything about caring for ethnic hair because the situation had never presented itself. Joy was pretty much bald until after her second birthday. I willed her hair to grow and applied growth products constantly, all to no avail. Amayah, however, had the most thick, beautiful, curly, dark hair, and I had no idea what to do with it. Thankfully, Jashanna was gracious enough to educate me about the best products and proper care. Jashanna loved to do her daughter's hair and would often spend a good deal of her visit time doing so. I didn't understand it at first. It looked to me like she was avoiding interaction with her child, but I began to see that this was one way she could connect with Amayah. I loved Amayah's hair wild and "natural," but to Jashanna and the culture she came from, it looked unkempt and undone. So I began to watch tutorials and learn easy styles for Amayah's hair that Jashanna would sweetly compliment me on, even though we both knew she could do far better. Still, it was important that I practice and do what I could with Amayah's hair because it was culturally important to her momma and to her. Therefore, it was important to me.

Joy struggled with Amayah. Peer relationships were uncomfortable and difficult for her. Joy loved her like a sister, but her trauma caused her to fight for control—and you and I both know how difficult it is to control a two year old! I could write an entire book on the control battles that went on in those short months when Amayah was a part of our family—and she was very much a part of our family. We view every child who comes to our door through foster care as a part of our family no matter how long they might be with us. We eat meals together, we pray over them, and we sing "Jesus Loves Me" before bed. We kiss and bandage them up when they fall down just as we do with all of our children. We have a wall in our home; it's my favorite wall in the house because it proudly displays our family pictures—pictures of our forever kids as well as the ones we were family to for just a little while. Our foster children are a part of our family story forever, and we are, forever, a part of theirs.

Amayah and Joy celebrated a birthday together that year with a sweet party that included friends and family. They wore their matching fairy princess dresses that my Mom (Mimi) made them for Halloween, and they played as little girls should. Tears flooded my eyes as Amayah opened a present with a baby doll inside and immediately began to cradle and rock it. This precious girl who came to us scared and unable to play had just picked up a doll and played with it appropriately! My mom and dad, who are sensitive to treating every grandchild the same, bought double of everything in an attempt to avoid fights between the girls. Kevin joked that it looked like our living room threw up pink everywhere. The birthday party was a beautiful view of family rallying around each other, coming together and loving whoever entered their world.

As it would turn out, Amayah never returned home to Jashanna. In our limited experience with foster care, there was still so much we didn't know. We did not know we had the option to keep Amayah with us, so we let her go when we could have and would have held on. The first time I met Amayah's soon-to-be adoptive parents, we seemed to have an instant connection. I liked them very much. I shared everything we had learned and witnessed about this beautiful girl they were setting eyes on for the first time. I shared the challenging things as well as the rewarding things about her because I didn't want them to walk into life with Amayah blindly. The last thing I wanted was for them to welcome this girl so dear to my heart into their home, realize they couldn't handle her, and later turn her away. Together, we created a plan that we thought would provide the best transition for Amayah. It began with a short visit at our home, and then a few days later they would take her out to a fun dinner—just the three of them. From there, visits would continue at their home and eventually to overnight stays. It was a gradual process meant to ease the transition for Amayah, and, I hoped, for our family as well. Really, though, how do you ease a goodbye to a child you love? Eventually, we found this lengthy goodbye to be more difficult on all of us, and we abandoned the plan in order to move Amayah to her forever home more quickly.

When people find out that we are foster parents, I hear more than anything, "Oh, I could never do that because I couldn't give them up." I know this comment comes from an innocent place, but it tends to strike me as a jab—as if I am so heartless that I *can* love a child and then let them go. The truth is that none of us can do it easily. It is excruciating, heart-wrenching, unbearable pain that we must bear for these children we love. We don't do it because we can; we do it because we must, and sometimes because that is what is best for the child.

Amayah would be the first little one who came to us through foster care who we would have to say goodbye to this way. We didn't have a frame of reference for what this transition would feel like, and, looking back, that was our saving grace. Our ignorance kept us isolated from the pain to come. We had no idea how much our hearts would hurt with this goodbye. We prepared Amayah and our family the best way we could. Our closest friends and family came to send her off and pray over Amayah and her future. We made her a picture book of our time together so she could take physical reminder of a family and a time in her life that she will not fully remember. Even today, the thought of a child I mothered for a time who won't remember me breaks my heart, and I don't think the Amayah hole in my heart will ever be filled.

Our last day with Amayah was a family day. I made pancakes for breakfast—the really special kind with mini chocolate chips in the batter—and shaped them into fun characters. We lingered at the breakfast table longer than usual knowing this would be our last meal together. We wanted something tangible that would help our children remember each other, so we went to *Build a Bear* where they all made the same Amayah bear. Her bear had a heart from all of us that we hugged and kissed, and our kids' bears all had a heart that Amayah had put in with love. Dropping our daughter off at her new home was one of the most difficult things I have ever done. I took her by myself, fearing that the emotions would be too overwhelming for all of our kids. I couldn't cry because Amayah needed me to be strong, she needed me to assure her that she was going to a wonderful place with a new mommy and daddy who would love her oh-so-much and that she would be happy there. I knew, without a doubt, that this family would love Amayah completely, but it did not dampen the hurt. I hugged her a little too tightly one last time and drove away, parking just around the corner because I was crying too hard to drive.

The house was much too quiet after Amayah left. The little girl who came to us so sad, so scared, and without smile had left a vacancy that was palpable. If you had met her shortly before she left our home, you would question everything I have written. Her great big smile brightened her face and the faces of those in her presence, her laugh was contagious, and she no longer anchored herself to me. In fact, thanks to Kevin's patience, by the time she left us, Amayah and Kevin had become the sweetest of friends, and she even preferred his company to mine. He was the first "daddy" Amayah had, and his positive impact on her paved the way for her to have a beautiful relationship with her forever daddy.

We didn't see Amayah for more than two years after that. Not seeing her, not knowing how she was doing, was even more painful than the initial goodbye. It broke my heart continually. It sounds crazy, I know, but sometimes if I was out in a crowded place I would look for her, longing to glimpse her great big smile once more to know that she was thriving. Amayah became the one that got away, a void in our hearts and our family who was intensely missed.

We stayed in touch with Jashanna and continued to show love

and support for her. The more we were involved in her life, the more we saw the lack of connection she had—to anyone. When Jashanna finally graduated with her GED after mustering the courage to go back to school, no one showed up to celebrate with her except us. It assured me that our place in Jashanna's life was needed, right, and good. I had the feeling that if we hadn't done anything else in our life, the love we showed Jashanna was something we did right. We took her out to *Chili's* that night and enjoyed what she said was the nicest restaurant she had ever been to. We encouraged her and celebrated her dreams for the future.

After years of longing to see Amayah, we heard from her family, and we were invited to slowly become a part of their lives again. The first time we saw Amayah after years of longing to see her face, my stomach ached as much as my heart soared. It's a strange thing seeing a child who you once mothered, who you have an in-depth history with, but who doesn't really know you anymore. Watching Amayah with her family, with her new sister she was growing up with, was all the assurance we needed that she was loved so incredibly well, and she had a great mommy and daddy who would forever take care of her and fight for her heart. This couple, this entire family, have become dear friends of ours, and our hearts are filled with gratitude every time we are together. Just weeks ago, we got together at a local park, and I marveled at the privilege of seeing Amayah laugh and kick her feet back and forth to swing with that gorgeous smile lighting up her face. I will be forever grateful for a place, any place, in Amayah's life. When it was time to leave, she and Joy walked out hand in hand, and I marvelled at their stories—both of them so different, so difficult— but I believe this chapter that we find ourselves in right now is becoming a thing of beauty.

Forever In My Heart

Although I'm not their mother
I care for them each day.
I cuddle, sing, and read to them
And watch them as they play.
I see each new accomplishment,
I help them grow and learn.
I understand their language,
I listen with concern.
They come to me for comfort,
And I kiss away their tears.
They proudly show their work to me,
I give the loudest cheers!
No, I'm not their mother,
But my role is just as strong.
I nurture them and keep them safe,
Though maybe not for long.
I know someday the time will come,
When we will have to part.
But I know each child I cared for,
Is forever in my heart!

Author Unknown

Emalee

"An older sister is a friend and defender—a listener, conspirator, a counselor, and a sharer of delights. And sorrows too."

Pam Brown

The phone rang unexpectedly at 10:30 in the evening on a Wednesday night, and the number on my screen's display was all too familiar. I picked up the line and began a comfortable banter with the placement specialist on the other end who we had come to know only by name and the sound of his voice. He told me about a sweet set of sisters who had been removed from their home earlier that day, explaining that the team had been trying to find an open home all day to keep them together. Regrettably, the agency was not able to find a home for four siblings. This happens because there is not a large enough pool of foster parents, and homes may already be full, not to mention that four extra children in one home is a lot, and many families do not feel up to the task. Eventually, they found a home for the older two sisters and decided to split the younger two up. They were calling me to care for the youngest of the sisters—the baby. My heart broke for these girls who were already experiencing so much trauma and then being split apart from each other. I asked if both sisters could come to our home, even if one had to sleep on the sofa. I begged them not to split up the youngest two. However, our license would already have to be amended to take the youngest. We simply did not have room to meet foster care codes for the baby's sister, and they already had a home for the older sister's arrival.

Just after midnight, a van pulled up to our front door. Kevin and I watched from the window as the social worker unbuckled an adorable child. As we opened the front door, we saw a terrified and exhausted baby. All I could do was imagine what this day had been like for her. Something undoubtedly scary had happened, and before long people showed up who she had never met before.

They took Emalee and her three sisters with them and away from their home, but at least they were together. They played in an office all day with new toys. Emalee wondered where her mom was, but she felt safe and was having fun playing with her sisters. Then it got late, and the people told the girls they were going for a car ride. Emalee expected that the van would take them home, but it stopped at a house she had never seen before. That's when the screaming and commotion started. The people were taking her two older sisters, and they did not want to go; they didn't want to leave Emalee and their other sister behind. Eventually, the people won, and Emalee's sisters were taken out of the van and left behind at an unfamiliar home—the home of strangers. Then, the same thing happened with her other sister and eventually to Emalee.

It was late, certainly well after bedtime for such a little one, but we couldn't put this terrified child right to sleep. Knowing what would comfort a child who just entered your home after receiving very little information about them was always a challenge. Thankfully, a warm bath with some lavender oil calmed Emalee followed by a bottle. (I know, I know—a child her age is too old for a bottle, but I didn't know if she had transitioned to a cup, and I knew that the sucking reflex is very soothing. This sweet child needed all the soothing she could get that night.) After some cuddles and lullabies, we finally got Emalee to bed. By this time it was well after 2:00 in the morning, with a house full of sleeping kiddos who were not aware we had grown by one overnight. The next morning, the sun rose, and with it rose our kids. We found their response to Emalee just like their response to all of the kids that came before her. I cannot say enough about what foster care has taught our kids and how it has shaped them—how it's shaped all of us. I'm immensely aware that had we not begun a journey in foster care, it would have been us who lost—lost the chance to know these amazing kids and their families and lost the chance for our eyes to be opened to all that love truly is.

We quickly learned that Emalee was scared of everything from our friends' fluffy, white, and completely harmless dog, to the doorbell ringing, rain falling from the sky, butterflies, and everything in between. Her speech was significantly delayed, with only a couple of words in her vocabulary that were barely recognizable, so we immediately got to work on evaluations for therapy. Unfortunately, beginning therapy for a child in foster care always comes along with hoops to jump through and a significant amount of waiting, when all we wanted to do was provide help and healing. We also got connected with her sisters' foster families to keep them close as much as possible, although they were currently living apart. We met at restaurants, had play dates, even sleepovers, and we took a lot of pictures to capture the connection they had. The four sisters loved each other—that much was clear—but there were some oddities, such as the older two not knowing the younger two children's names and referring to them only by vulgar nicknames. The older two sisters behaved in a "too grown-up" way and exhibited street smarts beyond their years. They had been used as makeshift babysitters; their parents had expected elementary age girls to take care of their siblings—the life they had lived caused these girls to grow up too quickly. They needed to be kids for a little while.

Initially, we were pretty confident that the two younger sisters who shared the same father would go home to him. Latasha and Emalee were about as many months apart in age as Emalee was old, and they needed each other—that much was clear. Latasha's foster parents were first timers and did not know when they first got the placement call that their foster license, which was for only one child, could be amended to two in order for siblings to stay together. We considered moving Emalee to their home early on, but because we expected that they would go home to their dad, we didn't want to cause more trauma with another needless move. There was significant time and energy spent keeping Latasha and Emalee connected to each other, which was easy because both foster families enjoyed the time we spent together.

Emalee's sweet momma was a broken woman stuck in a tragic cycle of substance abuse. I don't believe I ever saw or spoke to her when she was sober. I wanted to shield little Emalee from this side of her momma, but I suspected this was all she knew of her mom, regardless. It is my understanding that Emalee's momma wasn't always an addict. Emalee's momma was once strong and confident, ready to take on the world and make it a better place for her kids. But she was stuck in a segregated city and cycle of poverty. She did the best she could and was determined to break the cycle for her children's sake. Emalee's momma doted on her three small children. It was clear that they were her pride and joy, and the baby was something even more special. However, in a series of deeply horrific events over just a few short years, Emalee's mom lost two pregnancies, and it changed her. She would never recover from the ache of the babies who should be there.

I wonder what life for Emalee's momma and her babies might have looked like if she had been given support prior to these heartbreaking losses. Losing one baby is enough to affect you the rest of your life, but losing two pregnancies would be debilitating for any momma. For a mom so set on making things better for her children, on rising out of poverty and living a fully integrated life, there was promise. Yet, I imagine Emalee's momma felt unseen, like she was on an island of her own needing to provide and create change for her kids. What if the community had seen her and rallied around her? What if a state program or the neighborhood around her had stepped in to help her succeed instead of stepping in only after she failed? Life for Emalee's momma and her children might have looked very different. Tragically, for Emalee's momma, help came too late and she no longer had the heart, will, or the know-how to help her children or herself.

Emalee was a sweetheart. She was, generally, extremely happy and easygoing. Because she was younger than Joy, and thus less of a peer and more of a sister, Joy did significantly better with this placement. In fact, Joy actually relished the big sister relationship she found herself in once again. I remember the first time we took Emalee with us to church, all dolled up in a pretty dress that Joy helped pick out, with the girls in matching headbands and hair puffs. They walked into church hand in hand as Joy introduced her to everyone as her new sister. Emalee was good for Joy and Joy was good for Emalee. They needed each other for completely different reasons connected to a related background that the two of them seemed to understand, although it was beyond their years or level of comprehension to express.

Days quickly passed into months with five children in the house, three of whom were receiving various types of therapy, and the days became a blur. At this point in time we had a one, two, three, five and nine year old. I loved seeing people's eyes widen in surprise that sometimes looked more like horror when I shared our kids' ages. We were a diverse bunch, and my heart warmed every time I would hear a stranger compliment the beauty of our family. This happened more often than not, and many times I knew that, for a stranger, it was difficult to process. I would beam with pride every time with thanks and appreciation that they saw the same beauty that I did in my children. On the other hand, we experienced something terrible that is deeply burned in my memory to this day, partially because of what happened, and partially because of my shock and naivety in response to it.

I was at the grocery store with the three littlest ones while the Big Boys finished school. (When you have a large family, you go shopping when you have the least number of children with you.) It was a beautiful day in early summer when the air was filled with new warmth and the excitement of all of its potential. The kids were extra cheerful that day. When we entered the grocery store, Joy spotted one of those carts that looks like a little car and was thrilled to get a chance to drive it. She and Emalee were in the children's seats, each with their own steering wheel, having a great time, and our little guy was in the infant seat with a big smile, cooing away. They were making noise—that can't be denied—but it was the cheerful, happy noise of kids being kids and having fun. I turned the corner of the produce section, and before I knew what hit us, a middle-aged man wearing plaid and disgruntled face shouted, "Would you shut those niggers up?!" My jaw dropped in complete shock; I instinctively covered the baby's ears with pretend earmuffs and quickly looked around to see if there was anyone coming to our aid. Surely, someone would come to defend these sweet, beautiful children against this despicable word and ignorant man, but there was no one. It seemed, in this moment, that it was just the five of us in an otherwise empty store. I wanted to have the correct and immediate, even jabbing response, but all I could say in my shock and horror was, "Excuse me, they are just kids, and you may not talk to them like that." His response? "Well, niggers is what they are."

How do you respond in a situation like that? What can you say to an angry man to change his view? Even typing this disgusting word feels reprehensible. How do I protect my kids from this kind of treatment? Shaking, I quickly got out of that grocery store, leaving a full cart in an empty aisle and telling these three beautiful babies how special, wanted, loved, and cherished they were.

Dumbfounded that in my modern suburban setting there was still such racism and hatred, I saw an issue around me that I hadn't previously acknowledged. Suddenly, I saw the lack of diversity and it hurt, hurt for my kids who couldn't look around and see anyone who looked like them, and hurt for a culture so closed off from those who are different from them that they are missing out. If I ran into this man again today or found myself in a similar experience, I'm not sure what I would change in my response. Our words hurt—that's a fact—but rarely do words change people. My response to the hatred in our world is not to shield my children from it, but rather to foster love and acceptance of everyone, different and alike.

Emalee was growing and thriving. We continued to keep her and Latasha well connected, so much so that Joy thought for a time that Latasha was also her sister. If there was any real challenge with Emalee, it was her fears. In the months she had spent with us adjusting, she simply could not let go of her fears. It wasn't long before it became clear that Latasha and Emalee would not be able to return home to their dad, and we found ourselves at a crossroads. We adored Emalee, she fit well within our family, and we would have loved to watch her grow up as our daughter—forever. Still, how could we adopt her and keep her separated from her sister? We agonized over this, but ultimately decided that we could not look at Emalee one day and tell her we did not allow her to grow up with her sister. In the end, once again we found ourselves choosing our pain over the pain of the child we loved.

Saying goodbye to yet another child who came to us through foster care was debilitating because we knew what we were in for; we'd been through it before, and we remembered what that goodbye felt like. I was a weepy mess with every last moment we experienced with Emalee. I cried the last time we went to the zoo as a family, I sobbed the last time I sang "Jesus Loves Me" to her and put her to bed for the last night, taking in the sweet smell of her, and I blubbered all over the place the last time I did her hair and dressed her in a cute new outfit for her new home. We continued all the goodbye traditions we'd done with the other kiddos we'd said goodbye to and found some solace in the ritual of it all. It both broke my heart and filled me with relief that my kids had learned to say goodbye so well.

When the day of Emalee's move arrived, we packed all of the kids in the van and drove for nearly an hour to Latasha's house. Although we were heavy-hearted seeing her go, we knew this was a happy goodbye since she was being reunited with her sister. It was a quiet, somber ride while we all tried to process our powerful emotions. As we pulled up to the house, the first thing we saw was Latasha looking out of the window, jumping up and down because her sister was finally home! Emalee took my hand and led me through the house, showing me where her new room was and the new bedding she had picked out on a recent visit. She then led us outside to show us the slide and her new playhouse, all the while holding tightly to my hand and my heart. It was as if she needed to show me all she was gaining in this goodbye as much as I needed to see it.

Just days later, I received an update from Emalee and Latasha's mom with the most precious picture of Emalee snuggled up next to their big boxer dog. (You might remember that when Emalee was with us she was scared of everything, including our fluffy, white, wouldn't-hurt-a fly-puppy.) The girls' mom shared with me that with her sister by her side, Emalee was not scared of anything! She also shared that with Emalee there, Latasha began speaking at age level and fell right back into her role as big sister. We knew these sweet sisters needed each other, but this picture provided a tangible image of that. Seeing the sisterhood of Latasha and Emalee restored and all that they gained being back together where they belonged lessoned our pain tremendously. When the ache of missing Emalee threatened to overtake me, I remembered a scared little girl, merely a baby, who came to us having lost everything, and I am grateful to have been a part of giving some of that back to her. Two sisters are together today. Whole, healthy, sharing everyday moments, and supporting each other. Being a part of that reunification is something I will never regret.

Michael

*"The right thing to do and the hard thing to do
are usually the same."*

Steve Maraboli

Michael came to us unexpectedly, and honestly, I was emotionally unprepared. I was tired, and our family was tired, too. But I couldn't say no to this precious little one because we were connected to his family, and they reached out for our help. We knew there was no answer other than yes.

This was not an easy placement. In fact, it was complicated. Foster care is not a matter of black or white. There is so much gray area, so many times when we wonder if we are doing the right thing. Our friends and family questioned whether or not we could handle another kiddo in the home, and to be honest, I questioned it, too. But with this little one, we watched his parents dote over him, and we invited them into our home as an extended part of our family. Although they were unable to keep him safe at that time, their love for him was extremely evident. We knew that we were doing the right thing by stepping in and helping when they needed it.

Michael was one of the sweetest little guys, and he had a cheerful disposition. He was easy to care for, and our brood of kids loved having him around. With Michael, we developed a relationship with his parents, but it certainly did add some extra emotional weight and complications to work through. But by now we had a great deal of practice with the complicated and emotional.

Some of the other kids in our house were struggling significantly at this time, and I worried about how they would handle all of this. I shouldn't have worried considering the way the kids in our home have welcomed kids in the past. Never have they questioned why another kid was in the home or why we kept saying yes. None of them complained that they would have to share their toys, room, or parents with yet another child. They just stepped in to help and to love Michael as if they had done this a hundred times before. (Well, close to, anyway.)

Michael and his parents taught us that we always have more to give. However, we still needed to be careful to only sign up for what we could handle. And there is value in knowing that you can only do it with the help of the divine. It's God providing a calm over your heart and your home, it's a neighbor bringing a meal or sitting with you as you process what you're doing. It's your village holding you up when you get too weary.

It's exhilarating to do what we think we cannot do. It makes us more dependent on our God and our people, it takes strength that we didn't know we had, and it causes us to realize it is not us at all—it is the One who holds us. I often hear well-meaning people say, "God will not give you more than you can handle," but I don't believe that to be true. I have seen God give us more than we can handle a dozen times over again, but each time He gives us the strength to do what we are meant to do. It is strength we did not have when we entered into foster care the first time or the fifth time and every time thereafter. We, on our own, do not have the strength. But the strength we need will be brought and given to us to do what we need to do today.

We lived in that day-to-day strength until it became increasingly clear that we, as a family, were off balance. The day one of the other kid's therapists suggested a new kind of therapy that would take extensive training for us as parents. My immediate response was, "I just don't have any time to give to that." I knew some changes would need to be made. Letting go of Michael felt like a failure. While I can't say I am fully there, I am learning to understand that knowing when it is time to make a change, knowing when you are in a place where you can't continue in the same way is a positive thing. I'm beginning to believe that failure isn't truly failure unless we avoid walking through it, feeling it, and accepting it. As I learn to accept my limitations and give myself grace, I find that I have more grace to give.

Manny

"To succeed, you need to find something to hold on to, something to motivate you, something to inspire you."

Tony Dorsett

Several years into fostering, during our bi-annual relicensing, our social worker made the comment that she felt we had a good amount of experience under our belts and was going to put us on the list to contact us for a variety of things. She added that it would be up to us to use our judgment about what we said yes to. I suppose this is what experience in foster care gets you, and I was okay with that. What we truly wanted was to be available for the "hard to place" kiddos. Shortly after that day we received a placement call, and I knew we were in for a challenge when the placement specialist said, "So I know this is a little different from what we usually call you for." She told me about a teenage boy who had spent much of his life in the system. He was motivated and on track to graduate high school, and he simply needed a safe place to land until then. Right from this moment, Manny tugged on my heartstrings.

Caring for a teenage boy on the verge of manhood wasn't a situation that Kevin and I had ever faced before, so I had to talk with him before I could give her an answer. I tried calling him at work but was unable to reach him. I knew that Manny would be tough to place, and if it wasn't us, he would likely end up in a group home, so I kept trying to reach Kevin, and he finally answered. I shared the information that I had been given, and because these were new and uncharted waters for us, Kevin asked me to get some follow-up information. When I called the placement worker back, she connected me to Manny's previous case manager who was able to thoroughly answer our questions that put us at ease about saying yes to Manny.

He did not enter our home like the little ones before him had.

He entered with the weight of the world on his shoulders and a toughness to him that I suspected was primarily a façade, walls built up over time to protect himself. As he walked through the door, Manny carried a single Rubbermaid tub that held his clothes, his paperwork, and his memories—his every belonging. Our Big Boys were eager to show him around the house and play video games, but Manny wasn't interested. He just wanted to be alone. We set up his bed while he stood against the wall without offering to help or uttering a word. After it was all set up, we walked out of the room to give him space to settle in, thinking surely by dinner he would be ready to engage a little more.

We had a birthday party planned that night for one of our best friends, Max, and Kevin decided that he would still go, and he'd take Manny along with him. That may have been the best move we made in those first days with Manny. It allowed him to connect with Kevin and also with some of the other guys at the party. For Manny to see that people cared about him just because he happened to show up to a birthday party with a guy he just met—a party for a guy he had never met—was incredibly impactful for him. This night affected him so powerfully that he brought it up many times over the months to follow.

Kevin and I consider ourselves pretty young, although as the years go by we are finding ourselves less and less so, and we feel the tide turning toward a slightly more seasoned phase of life. It really wasn't all that long ago that we were teenagers, though, was it? Some days it feels like yesterday—other days like lifetimes ago. At this point, our oldest son teetered on the edge of "teenagehood," so we were just entering the thrilling experience of parenting a teenager. We had no prior experience with parenting a teen, let alone one on of the brink of manhood. We knew that Manny would need a fair amount of independence, but we also wanted him to see what a healthy family looked like. Along with his case worker, we set very generous ground rules and curfew for Manny for the school week and Saturday. Sundays, in an effort to show him what we were all about, we asked him to stick around and engage in the family day with us.

We wanted to make the first Sunday with Manny a special one. We found out that he had never been bowling, so naturally we squeezed all eight of us into our minivan and headed to the bowling alley. That day, Manny got to see what we were all about: loving each other and others, but he told us that he wasn't quite buying it. He didn't believe that this was real or that any family enjoyed being with each other as much as we did. This hurt my heart, and I wanted to bring Manny into the fold and show him how wonderful family could be. That night, when we got home, the older boys found common ground with him in superheroes, and they connected over Manny's favorite *Flash* movie. I had high hopes that this thing was going to work, that Manny would accept our family, and that we would make a lasting impact in his life.

With so many variables in foster care, you never know for certain how long a child will be with you. But with Manny, we knew. Knowing that we had such a small window to connect with him and make an impression on his life felt daunting. We told Manny from day one that foster care or not, he had a place to stay with us and should he leave and need to come back, our door would still be open to him. Kevin told him that he would never blow up at him or kick him out, wanting him to feel a sense of security—times would come later when I thought he was trying to get us to blow up or kick him out, but he never succeeded in either.

Manny had a distressing background, and the more he was

with us, the more he opened up to us about it. Sometimes our kids' stories made me mad, but Manny's story just made me sad. He had been through so much it was almost unbelievable, like he was rehearsing a movie script, but it was his reality. It was his life. Considering all that Manny had been through, he handled it quite well and was fairly well adjusted. However, he did not fully acknowledge the trauma from his past and how it affected his daily living and the choices he made. As a momma parenting kids who experienced trauma for years, I recognized it in him. I saw how what he had experienced framed his daily struggles, his wins and his losses. I wanted to help Manny work through these things, but he would not lower his guard enough to let me do so.

Parenting teenagers is tough; parenting a teenager with a traumatic background who just came to you when you have no buy-in is doubly hard. Many times I wished God had brought us into Manny's life earlier so we would have more time, more opportunity to make an impact. Kevin and I know all too well the grim statistics about kids in a situation like Manny's; we know that the deck is seemingly stacked against them. I was afraid of what his future might hold and what our place in it might be, but his future was not mine to choose. I questioned why God didn't bring us together at the start of Manny's stay in foster care, but knowing that God doesn't make mistakes, I knew there was a reason he was with us now. As long as we were in Manny's life, there was hope that we could connect with him and make an impact in this tide-turning time.

One of our most meaningful experiences with Manny was the night he made a delicious Mexican dinner for our family. It had become quite the joke between us that we took him out for "fake Mexican food" and couldn't even pronounce "Chorizo" correctly.

Manny decided he would cook us an authentic Mexican meal and show us how it was really done. He made the most delectable steak and potato meal with tortillas. He even invited a friend to our home for the first time to join us. It was endearing to have him describe his favorite meal that his mom used to make, knowing the memory was filled with very mixed and troublesome emotions. It was the most vulnerable he had ever been with us, and it filled me with hope that he would accept our family and allow us to bring him into the fold.

That night, sharing a beautiful meal together was the high point. Unfortunately, the weeks to follow brought some lows, and it became clear that we were going about this thing all wrong. Manny had a family, and in his eyes didn't need another one. He was stuck in a system that he felt trapped in, and we were a part of that simply by association. Kevin and I had to find another way to reach this kid. In desperation, we attempted more of a mentorship role. If Manny wasn't open to us bringing him into the fold, hopefully we could at least connect with him on some level and still be a support system for him, even after he left. Manny's school wasn't on our side of town, so Kevin drove him to school every day, which strengthened their connection. They shared many meaningful conversations on the ride to school. Kevin has always been a wonderful dad and foster dad, but seeing the way he was with Manny made me love and respect him even more. It was incredible to see the way Manny responded to Kevin. It crossed my mind that this would perhaps be the greatest gift our family had to give to Manny.

People are often hesitant to foster teenagers because of the stigma attached to it. But we were able to share our wonderful experience with him, so people gained a better understanding of what the experience was actually like. Generally speaking, fostering a teenager was easier than a little one because the hands-on daily care is so much less. It was certainly a good fit for us at that stage of our lives. On the flip side, a teenager is less likely to be cuddly like a little one, and depending on their experience, may not openly express gratitude. The misconception that children are in foster care because they have done something wrong is unfortunately still common in spite of all the awareness that organizations like ours and so and many others have worked to shatter. There is a great deal of fear out there that welcoming a teenager into your home through foster care is welcoming in the unfavorable things they have experienced. Certainly the child carries their experiences with them, but what we have found is that the kids are there through no fault of their own. Children in foster care are just that—children who deserve safety, security, and love. That is everything they want. They may ask for these things in less than desirable ways because they don't know how else to acquire what they need. Still, we as foster parents have the life-changing opportunity to teach another way and show them that they are in fact worthy of love, safety, security, and a family to call home.

Manny needed a lot of encouragement to stay in school. He was really motivated to be on his own. While I know this is a typical attitude for teenagers, no doubt years spent in foster care with other people making decisions for him added to this feeling for Manny. We got involved with the school and told them about the Manny we knew, wanting desperately for them to see the potential we saw in him. It was an uphill battle since many of his teachers had already formed negative opinions about Manny, but we challenged them to see beyond that and join us in helping him become the best he could be. Every child needs caring adults in their lives to help them succeed, and the more we could do that for Manny, the better.

After many years spent fostering children, I was the first foster parent who attended court with Manny. Participation in court dates is not mandatory for foster parents, but it is encouraged, and I've always viewed it as an opportunity to show the child and all the key players connected to them that we are invested. It pained my heart to think of Manny never knowing that support and to think of him as a young child just entering care, sitting in a cold courtroom all alone. The court date was on a weekday morning. Once we finished, I drove him back to school and found him more talkative than usual. Typically, on car rides with me, Manny immediately puts his ear buds in, and we sit in silence. But not that day. Rather, Manny kept a conversation going with me, but it was what he *didn't* say that spoke the most to me—it was his way of thanking me for showing up at court, for being there for him.

Manny had never celebrated a birthday. He went through his entire childhood without a birthday party, cake, or presents—things that we think are commonplace for a child to experience. We knew we couldn't let another birthday pass without Manny having his own party, but we also recognized that crowds and some of those typical family experiences made him nervous. Ultimately, we made plans with Manny's caseworker who he was very close with for a bowling party. We found it only fitting since this was one of the first things we did with Manny, and he was preparing to move on from our home. The party was simple and fun, filled with the things Manny's birthday should have been filled with every year prior. Kevin and I found ourselves, once again, filled with a range of emotions. There is a sense of value in being able to provide a person's first birthday party and a deep-rooted sadness that this was his first.

Our fear with Manny was that he would walk away from foster

care and from us at some point. For a teenager who experiences emotional ups and downs as a result of traumatic experiences, this was a real concern, and it frightened us. We were proud of Manny for sticking it out. We still worry, as all parents do for Manny, but we are honored to have been a part of the progress he made.

I want to tell you that his story ends well, but it doesn't. It was a difficult placement for our Big Boys who were most aware of the way his experiences alienated him from us. It was a difficult placement for us because we were never sure we had made the impact on him the way we wanted to, felt we needed to. There was no long goodbye with Manny; it was as if he was here one day and gone the next. We stay in touch and continue to assure him that our home and our family are always here for him, that we love him, we believe in him and are pulling for him. I rest in knowing that we gave Manny everything we could, and he knows he has a support system in his corner that he can tap into if he needs it. We can't dictate how anyone lives their life, but we can keep showing up and walking with them in love, and with Manny that is where we will leave our mark.

The Big Boys

"I am not sure that you can be taught how to love. In many ways it is innate—just watch and see what small child effortlessly does. But you can be invited to it and reminded of it."

Rasheed Ogunlaru

Often times people ask me how fostering has impacted our Big Boys. They were only two and six years old when we began fostering, so the Big Boys have grown up knowing little else. I enjoy thinking back to the day we received the call about Joy, remembering that for months previous to the call they had been asking when "the little girl" would come live with us. Having no answers for their inquisitive minds, I did a lot of redirecting to prayer, encouraging them to ask God to help our hearts to be ready for this child when she needed a safe home. As I shared the news with our Big Boys about Joy coming to us, they were overcome with excitement and quickly ran into the room we had prepared while we waited, making sure everything was in its place. One of them even picked out a cute fuzzy set of pajamas for her to wear to bed. Their happiness in welcoming this baby girl was intoxicating.

Kevin and I spent a lot of time talking with the Big Boys leading up to this moment. We explained in age-appropriate terms why a child would enter foster care and what a foster family's role was. At this point, they were too little to fully understand foster care, but we did make it clear that this would be something the whole family had to agree on. We revisited this conversation often because we knew the day would come when they understood more and had a voice in the process. Although Kevin and I hoped to adopt, we never expressed that to our Big Boys, instead focusing on the temporary nature of foster care in an attempt to keep their hearts safe. We reminded them many times that a child would come to us because she needed a safe place for a little while so her family could heal. At this point we didn't know any other foster families, so we introduced the beauty of fostering to our Big Boys at our pre-placement classes where they got to see families who didn't look alike, but they shared a great deal of love for each other.

Unable to sit still as I waited for Joy, I put on a movie for the Big Boys, but I can't remember which one. I would love to be able to tell Joy, "this is the movie we were watching the day you came home," but I just can't. It was such a whirlwind of an experience that few details from that evening stick with me now. Our Big Boys cuddled up on our living room sofa so sweetly, waiting to meet the new baby we would welcome into our home and hearts instantly. When the doorbell finally rang, they were over the moon and couldn't wait to hold and snuggle Joy. Although her first night with us was extremely rough, it didn't stop our Big Boys from holding her and didn't damper their excitement of welcoming Joy to our home.

When Joy came to us, something changed in the Big Boys. Something wonderful. I don't know if it was having a little girl in the house for the first time enhanced by the fact that she was a tiny baby or if it was being a part of foster care, but regardless, they have never been the same. When Joy entered our home, it made the Big Boys even more compassionate, kind, welcoming, and giving than they already were. They began thinking less about themselves and more about others. At school, their teachers began to see something special in the Big Boys; they were given leadership roles in their classes because they could be trusted to help others. The Big Boys are still growing and learning and are in no way perfect, but they have a wonderful foundation to build on.

Each time a foster kiddo has left us, we've held a family meeting to process how much time we would need to mourn the goodbye and to recharge. Then we would decide, together, when we were ready for another child. It's imperative that we continue the conversation to ensure that we are all invested on this journey because Kevin and I are not just foster parents—our entire family fosters together. We are a foster family. At every family meeting such as this, the Big Boys have been with us and excited to welcome another child in. In fact, they love being foster siblings so much that after telling them a kiddo is leaving, their first question after shedding tears is, "when is the next one coming?" It has hurt them to say goodbye to the children they've welcomed in as siblings, but even so, our Big Boys continue to give their vulnerable hearts to each child who enters our home. Their resilience amazes me and pushes me to continue when the hurt feels too bad.

Sometimes our Big Boys have experienced other types of sadness because they understand a child's brokenness. When we see other people's hurt and pain, it's inevitable that it will impact us. Foster care, like life, has not always been a walk in the park and our Big Boys have seen that, felt that. In fact, our most recent fostering experience was hard on the Big Boys in many ways. If we only focus on this particular experience, it doesn't tell the story that I want it to. But foster care has never been about me, and I know deep in my heart that what we have done on this journey, even with our most difficult placements, we have done out of love, and we find solace in that. My momma heart wants to shield my Big Boys from all of the heartache in our world. Yet I know the reality is that we can't shield our kids from everything in life. What we *can* do is walk through the difficult stuff with them, giving them the tools and experience to make it through to the other side. When they do make it through, they receive the gift of an experience that helps them to walk in solidarity with others. My Big Boys are seeing the messiness of life. I believe they will continue to step in and show love no matter what. We don't understand what we don't know, and our they have come to learn and know a lot about themselves, what engaging in the brokenness of our world looks like, and what loving others looks like—an experience we would not trade for anything.

When I asked my Big Boys what foster care meant to them, they both chimed in with one word—family. They expressed that the children who have entered our home through foster care and the family connected to them have become one big extended family to them, and they love that. They said that foster care has taught them to love and accept everyone, even if they don't understand the choices they make. My Big Boys said the hardest part of fostering has been saying goodbye to the kids they welcomed in as siblings, telling me that they still miss them all of the time. They also shared that inviting a child in who has a different background and does things differently has, at times, been difficult to adjust to, yet it has taught them to be even more loving and kind.

There is something I love about watching a big sibling give a little one a piggyback ride, which is typical around here. With hint of nostalgia and a whole load of adorable, this sight can melt my heart quicker than a push-pop on a hot day. When I see the Big Boys hoist a "little" on their back and skip off to whatever activity lies ahead, I see childhood, family, and love without question. It's easy for us to love others who benefit us, but for us to love someone who we do not benefit from, even someone who emotionally drains us, is love on a whole different level. This is how I have seen my boys love through foster care. They have given up regular holiday traditions to welcome in the biological family of our foster kids. They have given up security in our family make up since it is always changing. Our Big Boys had to move to a smaller room or move things around in their own room to make space for a new child who needed a safe place to stay. They have endured meltdowns at breakfast, lunch, dinner, school events, and everywhere in between. Our Big Boys have given up some of their time so we can all spend time with a new child. Watching them love these siblings, sometimes for a little while, sometimes forever, shows me another glimpse of what love is meant to look like.

Grammy and Grandpa

"My father used to say that stories are part of the most precious heritage of mankind."

Tahir Shah

I was only three years old when my grandpa passed away; sadly I have very few memories of him. He was quite sick leading up to his death; consequently, the images of those days are the only memories I have of him. However, our family has kept his memory alive by sharing stories of him so much so that many of the stories I've heard over the years feel like my own memories. Stories of what my grandpa did and how he loved is how his legacy stays alive. My grammy passed away about eleven years ago after a heart-rending battle with Alzheimer's. The grammy we knew and loved disappeared before our eyes, leaving only a shell we barely recognized. She no longer knew her family—in fact, she didn't even know her own reflection. I remember one day, near the end, when I turned the corner to find my grammy eerily talking to herself in the bathroom mirror, tipping her head back and laughing at the woman she saw before her. It's an image that I wish I could unsee. It scared me and rocked me to the core—the image haunts me still. I try to forget seeing her like that and remember the grammy who loved to laugh with her family.

Grandpa spent many years as a carpenter. Really, though, he was a pastor and leader by love. He often led small churches that could not pay him and support his large family of seven, so he would accept payment in the form of fresh eggs, milk, or meat from nearby farms owned by his parishioners. Even now, years after their passing, if we run into people who knew them from church they will say, "Your grammy and grandpa came to love us." Grandpa was a man who earned respect from his children and those around him because of the way he lived. He never raised his voice, he was calm and collected, and he was steady. Grammy wore her heart on her sleeve; she was emotionally vibrant, loved to sing, laugh, and she adored babies. Grammy's smile expressed a beautiful spirit like no other. When I think of her now, I picture her in heaven sitting next to Jesus with her head against his shoulder, smiling ear to ear and singing the sweet songs of praise I grew up hearing. They raised their family as an authentic example of how to love others. Each of their grown children is living a life of love and service to others because that is what they were raised to do. This is my grammy and grandpa's legacy. This is the foundation of why I know what it is to love others today.

My dad grew up in a broken family. He didn't know his father well, and he only visited him a couple of times each year. He loved his father and his father loved him, but distance and lifestyle separated them. His mother loved him very much, but she struggled with some demons she could not rid herself of. Dad's mother would often go away for days or weeks at a time, leaving a scared little boy home to manage alone. This caused my dad to learn the art of survival, but never the real love and connection that family is meant to offer. Meeting my mom provided not only a love connection for dad, but also a family connection for the first time. Grandpa taught my dad the carpentry trade and offered him side jobs in the early years with great patience and grace, even when it meant rebuilding a staircase late after hours because my dad didn't get it quite right. He will tell you that my mom's family—my grandpa and grammy—taught him how to love and what family is. Just recently, when I listened to my dad explain his relationship with my mom's family and the way they welcomed him in, accepted him, and showed him what a family is meant to look like, it struck me that they served as his foster family. My grammy and grandpa gave my dad everything a foster family aims to give to the children who come into their home. They introduced him to the love of family; they showed up for him time and time again, and in this, dad began to learn to trust. How beautiful it is that seeing how others worked together as a family began with my grandparents. Kevin and I are not the first ones in our family to engage in foster care. My grandma and grandpa did that long before I was born, long before I was even aware of the healing power of family. How I wish they could see our family now; no doubt they would beam with glee over the love and fostering they sparked years ago, not knowing it would ignite a flame in me. This past summer we had a family reunion in South Dakota. It had been twelve years since I saw my mom's side of the family, so they had not yet met my little three, my adopted kiddos. Grammy and grandpa are no longer with us, but I know without a doubt that they would have loved and accepted Joy, My Hero and Bubba as their own. I know this because my grandparents' legacy, my aunties and uncles and cousins, welcomed all of my children with open arms. One of my cousin's daughters wrapped up a beautiful doll to give to Joy because she was excited to have another girl cousin. Another one of the little cousins connected with Bubba so wonderfully that by the second day they had created their own special handshake. My little three were not born into this loud, crazy, loving family, but still, they are a part of my grammy and grandpa's heritage, which means they are not only recipients of their example of love, they will also learn to carry it out.

Our Village

"Too often we underestimate the power of a touch, a smile, a kind word, a listening ear, an honest compliment, or the smallest act of caring, all of which have the potential to turn a life around."

Leo Buscaglia

No one can walk this journey alone. We need each other to laugh with, to cry with, and to support each other. Kevin and I like to refer to our friends and family who are with us on this journey as "our village" that helps us raise up the children who enter our home. Even more so, they help raise *us* up when the struggle starts to wear us down. Our village is a vital support system that we could not do without. Every foster family needs a support system like our village. If you have a passion for those involved in foster care but are unable to be a be a foster parent yourself, get connected with a family who is and provide support. Or maybe you are a foster parent reading this, feeling as if you are on this journey by yourself. To you I say, "Reach out." Share what it feels like to be foster parents with your friends and family, and express what they can do to support you. Plan a grown-up only game night, invite some friends and laugh together, ask for help providing needed items for that new little one, or reach out for a meal on a particularly busy night. It will do a world of good for you as well as the friends and family who you bring on this journey with you.

Joy came to us with very few clothes and supplies. Her caseworker, who was one of the best we've had, went shopping for a few outfits and a blanket. When you become a licensed foster parent, it is typically for an age range. Ours was newborn to three years, and I wasn't prepared for all that it meant. While we waited for the placement call, I saw adorable little girls' clothing everywhere I went and had to restrain myself from buying all of it. Girls are just more fun to shop for than boys! Joy came on a Wednesday evening close to bedtime, and by morning my sister was there with a meal and a large bag full of the most adorable tiny baby girl clothing.

She lovingly picked each outfit, and she even included an itty-bitty, colorful dress for Joy's first Sunday at church.

My sister is an extremely busy and involved mom of three. She has teenage twins (a girl and a boy) and a son in elementary school. There are a variety of special needs in their family, and my sister is a constant advocate for their needs. When Joy needed an Individualized Education Plan, or IEP, she talked me through the paperwork and even attended the meeting with me, there every step of the way. Her knowledge and experience brought me peace as I navigated the unknown waters. She is a middle school French Teacher, on the PTA board, a Sunday School Teacher, Girl Scout leader, and an Autism Therapist. That's right! She is one tenacious, fascinating woman who does it all. In spite of the many hats my sister wears and the busy schedule she keeps, she is the kind of person who will drop everything to help a friend or family in need, which I have seen her do time and time again.

My sister has been one of my greatest supports as we've gone through this process. With every child who has entered our home, she has been there within hours to deliver needed supplies. Whether it be clothing, formula, age appropriate toys or bedding, she's purchased it and delivered it as needed. The best part is that I have never needed to ask her for any of this. My sister inquires about what each new child needs. She has also babysat our foster children more times than I can count. She will be the first to tell you that she is not in a place that she can foster, but she can definitely support us in the journey and love the children who come to us. Not only has she supported us with clothing, supplies, and babysitting, but she also has been Auntie to all of the kids who enter our home. The way she loves these children is no different from the way she loves her biological nieces and nephews. I'm eternally grateful to have an extended family to give to the kids who enter our home through foster care. Being loved by my sister and the rest of our village is a priceless gift.

Another priceless member of our village is Jolie. She began helping us with the "littles" while we were serving in our church's youth department several years ago. I'm not sure how she was recruited for this job, but I was thrilled that she was. Jolie had previously been our oldest son's Sunday School teacher, and we held her in high regard as his favorite teacher ever. She is the kind of woman who is not easily ruffled and knows how to have a good time—attributes that were certainly needed since she would be caring for six kiddos from two families, most of whom were with us via foster care. Jolie connected with each of our kids immediately and individually. She played games with those who enjoyed competition, she brought crafts to do with the kiddos who needed more calming activities, and she rocked and cuddled the babies in sweet comfort. Our kids could not wait for Wednesdays when they got to see Ms. Jolie! As if helping us on Wednesdays was not enough, Jolie offered to babysit anytime we needed. She became our go-to babysitter because we knew she could handle our brood. Even more, we knew that they would be well-loved and have a great time while she was with them. Jolie has become something like a sister or an auntie to me, we all love her like family, and she spoils the kids rotten like a Grandma would (although she's much too young to be their Grandma). She sends them back to us surged up, with arms full of gifts, and hearts full of love.

Two years ago, Jolie told us she would be moving out of state. I mourned and stayed in denial for a long time. She wasn't going to move until her house sold, so I often found myself between praying her house wouldn't sell so she could stay and praying that it would because I knew she was excited about this new job. Jolie invited us to come do a walk through of the house and "take what we wanted" before she began purging. It was then that I could no longer deny what was happening. It felt irreverent to be walking through her home and picking what I wanted to leave with; at the same time I wanted some tangible things to remember her by. For years, Jolie had been generously giving to our family, and that day she one-upped herself by giving us the kitchen table that had been in her family for generations. She even prepared a tasty meal for dinner. It was the first time since beginning foster care that we had a table large enough for our entire family to sit at; it was the first time in years we shared a true family dinner.

We keep in touch with Jolie and miss her desperately. I'm thankful for technology that allows us to share pictures and videos as easily as phone calls. She is still very much part of our lives. This past Christmas, she was in town visiting, and true to Jolie fashion, she showed up with a Santa Claus bag full of gifts for our kids—all of our kids, including our newest foster son! To me, the best gift was seeing her, wrapping her up in hugs and seeing the excitement on our kids' faces as she walked in. When it was time to say goodbye again, we did so with tears welling in the corners of our eyes, trying not to let them escape. But we said goodbye with hearts full, knowing that near or far, Jolie was family and she meant the world to us.

Our incredible friends Mariah and Luke have been on this foster care journey with us since day one. In fact, before they got married, Mariah was living with us when we received our first placement call—the call for Joy. Because she was not an approved caregiver or member of our household, I had to make a difficult phone call to Mariah telling her we were welcoming in a baby girl, so she had to move out. Imagine making that call to one of your best friends, telling her she had to be out of your house almost immediately, and most certainly that night . . . but Mariah took the news well, knowing that this was a journey God had called our hearts to do. We were finally getting the opportunity to walk out this heart-placed passion. Mariah wholeheartedly shared in our excitement that day and has been there with us for the hardships and delights every day since.

Luke and Joy shared a special bond from the day they met. Maybe it was a result of sharing the same hairstyle (bald!), or maybe Joy connected to his fun loving nature. I remember a time when Joy was still a baby, and Luke was playing with her, holding her up above his face, making her laugh with his silly facial expressions. Without warning, she responded to him by spitting up—that's right, you guessed it—in his mouth! Instead of sprinting away screaming, he stuck around, and what could have been a disgusting moment actually solidified their bond. We joke to this day that they are friends forever because if you spit up in someone's mouth and they still want to be friends with you, you know you've found a good thing.

These friends have been incredibly involved and present in our lives; they are a constant for us and for our kids. Their friendship and support, even on a journey that they have not experienced, has been so necessary for our survival. Luke and Mariah have played vital roles in the lives of a foster family; they've played the role of friend, of confidant, of support system . . . and oh, the much-needed laughter we've shared over the inside jokes we have and times around the kitchen table playing *Scatagories* or *Mexican Train Dominoes*. Recently, Mariah made a comment about the day when Joy came home to us. (Remember, that was also the day we lovingly kicked her out of our house.) Mariah said that welcoming Joy into our lives changed us *all.* You see, Luke and Mariah were changed because Joy not only came into our lives—she came into the lives of our friends and family. Today they are loving and mentoring a neighbor girl who has spent years in the foster care system and has little support. They know we each have a role to play and an impact we can make on kids and families in care.

Heather was on the legal team for one of our cases. I met her in the courtroom the first time she came to present the state's case. From the foster parents' assigned seat in the back of the courtroom, I saw a woman who exuded compassion and grace, and I could not wait to meet her. We talked in a crowded hall for a mere three minutes, but I saw her heart, that she understood the reality of kids in foster care and the family members connected to them. Heather genuinely wanted what was healthy and safe for everyone involved in her cases. She wanted the best for Joy, and regardless of what that would be, I knew she would fight for and do right by this special child who had entered her life and mine.

When our case hit the "Termination of Parental Rights" phase, Heather was my go-to for the millions of questions I had. When I was worried about the outcome, she talked me down off of the ledge and gave me the facts. Heather explained the process to me countless times to ensure that I understood what was happening and what would be coming next. On trial day, Heather sat with me outside the courtroom and calmed my nerves with her sweet spirit and grace-laced truths before I took the stand to testify. In addition, when TPR was granted, she celebrated all that meant with us while also mourning the reality of the loss associated with it.

Heather was present for our first adoption day along with at least fifty friends and family who walked the journey with us. We packed that courtroom, and I felt as if there had never been a more joyous session in court. You can always tell the adoptions from the other cases at family court because kids are dressed in their Sunday best. Heather, as if she had not already given enough, brought a sweet and perfect gift that is treasured to this day. Heather was assigned to another one of our cases. We knew that we were safe with her, our kids were safe with her, and we breathed a little more easily knowing that she would fight for what was right and what was fair without bias because that is who she is. Heather is truly one of the most honorable people we know, so when she was granted a seat on the Judge's bench, we celebrated with her, knowing there was no one better for the job. I've often said that if I was going to have to sit before a Judge, I would want it to be one like Heather who would follow the letter of the law while also showing grace and providing an opportunity for my betterment.

In the most beautiful gift Heather could possibly give us, she presided over the adoptions of both Bubba and My Hero. Having a Judge who knows you, your family, and your children's stories perform their adoption is precious beyond all words. Heather has become a treasured friend of our family and no doubt someone we will continue to learn from.

Kevin and I like to say that everyone can do *something* in foster care. Some people are equipped to become foster parents and others to support families who do. Fostering has been the best thing we have done with our lives, but it is not without challenge and emotional weight. I am convinced we would not have been able to engage in foster care for as long or as well as we have without our village, our people alongside us to help lift our arms when the weight gets too heavy. Every time someone brings a meal or supplies to a foster family, every time someone offers to provide respite or babysitting, every time someone spends time investing in the lives of that family and their children, they do that "something" they can do. Your "something" goes a long way in showing love to our kids and to us, and it plays a vital part in the redemptive story of foster care.

My City

"Devote yourself to loving others, devote yourself to your community around you, and devote yourself to creating something that gives you purpose and meaning."

Mitch Albom

It has been named the fifth-poorest city in the U.S.[1] with nearly thirty percent living in poverty,[2] and it's been called the worst state in the country for racial differences between black and white children,[3] and it is labeled the most segregated city in the US.[4] It's statistics like this which make me think of Emalee's sweet momma and understand her situation all the more. It's foster care and getting to know the stories of our kids and their parents, beginning to understand and see them that has opened our eyes to the city. Sadly, when people think of Milwaukee, these claims and statistics distort the truth. I was one of those people for many years, comfortably living in my privileged suburban world away from the reality of what was transpiring in the city. It shames me to remember a time when I was afraid to drive down certain streets or go to certain areas.

Kevin and I liked nice things, and we enjoyed living in a well-landscaped, safe, and clean neighborhood. We spent our time with people who looked like us and lived like us without a second thought about it. I think back to when we began fostering and needed to travel to "those areas" for doctor appointments or visits and then getting out of dodge as quickly as possible. I remember a time in the waiting room for one of our little one's appointments in the city. The waiting room was extremely full, and patients

---

1   Sanburn, Josh. "This is the Poorest Big City in the U.S." TIME Magazine 17 Sept. 2015; based on US Census Bureau, American Community Survey 2014 data

2   United States Census Bureau / American FactFinder. "S1701 Poverty Status in the Past 12 Months" 2009 – 2014 American Community Survey. U.S. Census Bureau's American Community Survey Office, 2014. Web. 7 March 2016

3   Race for Results: Policy Report. Rep. Baltimore: Annie E. Casey Foundation, 2014.

4   Jacobs, Harrison, Andy Kiersz, and Gus Lubin. "The 25 Most Segregated Cities In America." Business Insider. Business Insider, Inc, 22 Nov. 2013.

were being called in on more of a lottery system than the time slot appointments I was accustomed to. I scanned the room and saw a woman having a conversation on her phone about a funeral she had attended the previous day for a friend who died of a gunshot wound. This was exactly the image I had of Milwaukee—a picture the media painted well—of constant deaths due to gun violence. And white suburbia was buying it. In my limited understanding, I was thankful that our kids were safely out of this environment, and I felt like we did them a favor of sorts.

As we continued to spend time involved in foster care getting to know the kids and families we were working with, we began to understand the impact of the privilege we came from. True, it was not a privilege we asked for, it was a privilege we unknowingly benefited from because of the color of our skin and the community we lived in. In addition, I began to see our children who came to us through foster care sticking out in the community; no one else looked like them, and this was not okay with me, but I wasn't sure what to do about it. At first, I tried to teach all of our kids about different cultures and celebrate the differences we all have. We began doing cultural dinners once a month in which we cooked food from other cultures and countries and learned about what they valued and celebrated. Our conversations then turned to social justice issues and concerns that we saw around us. This plan worked well for a while; we were proud of the open conversations happening in our home and the heart our kids displayed. But before long, it became clear that this was not enough. Please hear what I am NOT saying here. I am not saying that you can't engage in social justice or people and cultures who have differences from you living in the suburbs. Certainly there are many people doing this, for which I am eternally grateful. For us, however, we felt charged to live differently.

We heard about a great community working together in the heart of Milwaukee. One of the families, the Wilsons, hosted what they called "Family Dinner" every Thursday night for anyone who showed up—anywhere from twenty people to well over a hundred. Everyone was welcome, and the Wilsons served dinner on their own dime each week! If you ask them why, the Wilsons will tell you that they call it family dinner because it's like a family holiday once a week. It's a time for us all to enjoy real, loving community and an opportunity for the Wilsons to serve their neighbors. Our family spent many early summer evenings at family dinner amazed at the diversity we saw there and the love represented. We found that no one cared about the color of anyone's skin or their socio-economic status—they simply cared about each other as human beings, and they learned from each other's experience and differences. Family dinner is truly a remarkable display of doing life together in community.

More and more, as we spent time in this community, we felt our hearts break for our city and the people who lived there. It angered me that some people were scared to travel into the city for fear of the unknown and what they did not understand, even though I had felt that way once, too. It troubled my heart that I could drive down one single street and the closer I got to certain city markers, the more rundown and condemned it became. I didn't know what the solution was, but solidarity seemed like a good place to start. Kevin and I put our house, the quintessential "first home," an old white farmhouse that we had nursed back to its intended beauty, on the market. To our amazement, we had two offers by the end of the first day. It was time to find a house in the city, only when we began looking in the community we had come to love, we got cold feet and we were suddenly scared of the possible dangers and the unknowns. We looked everywhere else and put multiple offers in on other homes. When the doors to those offers didn't just close, they slammed in our face, God got our attention and we went back to the community we now knew without a doubt that God had called us to.

The day we moved into our city house, our friends and family were there to help us unload, and our new neighbors began showing up as well. It was the first time we saw the community rally around us, a sweet blending of our people, old and new. A block party followed our big move, and we felt instantly welcomed and at home, we jokingly asked if they threw a block party every time someone new moved to the neighborhood. The kids played the night away with new friends like they never had before. If you could see the amount of children on our block! Just between us and our neighbors directly on each side we have fourteen kids, all in similar ages, some of whom also share an adoption history. It's as if God hand-picked this home, this community, for us and us for it. The block party continued until the summer sun set, taking the last bit of daylight with it. We all fell into bed, exhausted from a day of unpacking and connecting with neighbors.

Several hours later I woke to the persistent buzzing of my phone—messages and texts from friends and family asking if we were okay and from new neighbors asking about the helicopters over our house. I turned on the news to images I would not be able to put out of my mind. It was our neighborhood engulfed in the flames of riots with angry people everywhere. If I am being completely honest with you, my first instinct was to run. My sister's house was just across the freeway from us. I could wake up the kids, load them in the car and head over to presumed safety. However, paralyzed by fear, I stayed up all night watching the news feed, feeling like the mob was closing in on us. My heart was racing, and I couldn't control my breathing. I was on high alert, petrified because I didn't know what I could do to keep my family safe in a situation like this.

They called it "unrest" sparked by yet another fatal police shooting, but it was a response to so much more than one incident. It was years of mistrust and misfortune, of unemployment, incarceration, poor education, and a sense that the black community in Milwaukee had been overlooked or forgotten. Rioting was not the answer, but what is the answer when a community has felt unseen and unheard for so long?

We were invited to attend the church in our new neighborhood the next morning. After service, they would walk to the park where most of the rioting took place, pick up trash, pray with whoever was there, and be a positive presence. As much as I wanted to stay holed up in the house all day, alone with my family and my fear, I knew that was not the healthy response, and the only way through this fear was to continue on in spite of it. Walking to the park with a slew of people I had never met before, we shared a commonality . . . a brotherhood and sisterhood coming together to display the beauty that was in our community, a community we just joined. I don't know if I felt more like a novice or a fraud, but I certainly struggled with the feeling that we didn't truly understand what had transpired the night before. We got to the park, and my heart stopped and set up camp inside my throat—the sight was magnificent. Hundreds of people, black and white, standing embracing or together hand in hand in prayer. The crowd at the park was claiming ground, and the ground was this community as a place of healing and reconciliation, a place to move forward together in love. I even saw a couple of friends from the suburbs who came to the park because they knew they could not just sit at home—they had to do something. It was an incredible moment, and I was honored to be a part of it.

The next night in our new home went much like the first. Our block was quiet, but I was fiercely aware that only blocks away things were not the same. It was another night of rioting, and the image of officers in full riot gear was intimidating. I sat, unable to take my eyes off of the news coverage, still fighting the fear and the instinct to flee. Kevin and I knew that if we moved into the heart of the city we would see things we didn't witness in the suburbs, and that we would have to process things differently. But I didn't expect anything like this. I sat, frozen in my fear, unable to sleep, asking why God had brought us here at a tumultuous and frightening time like this when God had impressed upon my heart that this was exactly why he brought us here. You see, along with the rest of the world, I was witnessing the worst of it covered by the news, further feeding into the stereotype of the city. Feeding the fear created a false understanding of what my city was all about. During that time of unrest, I saw Kevin and some of our neighbors praying with police officers as they began their shifts, other neighbors sitting with us as we processed with uneasiness what was happening around the corner, someone giving out "free hugs" at the scene of the rioting, and others bringing food and water to share. Community coming together stood out to me the most and it was clear this wasn't simply in response to the alarming activity happening around them, loving each other is the way this community and my city lives life.

Left with a decision to make, I knew that I could flee or I could fight where God had planted us and share the good around us as the world looked on. Kevin and I took the opportunity to provide a voice for the beauty we saw around us. At times it was as simple as a picture and post on social media bringing light to the beauty of our city. Other times we had incredible opportunities to share about Milwaukee with the media. We still have fears, but we don't highlight those fears, and that is how we disarm them. We choose to see and highlight the beautiful. This is our response and our charge, to our city, our home, to help bring light to the beauty around us for those who do not know and do not see.

This community hosts egg hunts for the kids at Easter, brings meals for neighbors when they are sick or return home from a vacation. This community allows our kids to grow up with a diverse group of people to learn from. Recently, our oldest Big Boy was over at our neighbor's house watching a show on racial issues in America with his friend who so happens to be of African decent. After the program, they discussed different experiences with these racial issues and spent time learning from each other. The Big Boys are growing up with eyes open, learning first hand what it took Kevin and I years to process. They will not grow up in fear of people who look or act differently from them. In fact, they will grow up learning to stand with their brothers and sisters of all races and backgrounds. I am eternally grateful that my three littles are growing up in a place where they can look around and see people who look like them. I'm aware that as the years go on they will have more to process because of their foster care and adoption history. However, this piece of who they are will be something they grow up knowing. We are currently teaching our kids about strong black individuals in history. The other day, Joy and I were reading a book about Harriet Tubman, and I realized that she, in her childhood innocence, had no idea what slavery was. For a moment I wanted to shield her from that awful part of our American history, but I knew there were lessons to be learned from the past. Explaining slavery to my child, who herself would have been a part of this despicable institution, was tough. I went on to connect that to the civil rights movement, which we have talked about many times before that. Joy's response was on par when she said, "Why would you treat anyone differently because the color of their skin? That doesn't even make sense." My sweet girl could not be more right on that one.

Our family has been well loved by our new community. We were quickly absorbed into a rotation of Wednesday dinners with neighborhood families, and this saved us. I don't know if we would've made it through the scary things in our community without the love of our friends. These dinners bring us together— some who share similar views to us, and others who stretch our viewpoint. Perhaps what I am most grateful for is the way our children have been brought into the fold. Neighbors have become precious friends to them. Recently, two of our neighbor families were gone on vacation, and they returned with souvenirs for our kids. I can tell you for a fact my children have never had friends like this before.

Just today my children and I took part in a community painting of a mural only a couple of blocks away. Neighbors came to do what they could and have a part in the creating the mural. The owner of the corner store nearby even invited the volunteers to come in for a free cold beverage. It was another beautiful example of the community coming together and an honor to take part in, an honor we may never have experienced if not for foster care. Learning from those both alike and different from you is truly the best way to live. I am convinced more than ever that we are created for community. Kevin and I are striving to live our lives intentionally; we are showing our kids that all people matter and we have a great deal to learn from each other, we are continuing to learn what it is to live and love well with our eyes wide open.

Social Workers

"Change will not come if we wait for some other person, or if we wait for some other time. We are the ones we've been waiting for. We are the change that we seek."

President Barack Obama

Initial Assessment Specialist, Licensing Specialist, Ongoing Case Manager, Family Preservation Specialists, CPS—you will find that social workers go by many titles depending on their area of specialty. Social workers have all gone to college intending to make a difference. Many go on to receive their Master's degrees, and yet the turnover rate for social workers is close to fifty percent. This is a difficult field of work, and burnout is understandable when you work in a broken system full of hurting people. It is not one person or one system's fault; a variety of social issues impacts the system. Understanding the issues and finding a solution is an extensive endeavor. Social work is an emotional job that all too often goes unseen and unappreciated. I cannot imagine the gut-wrenching nature of this type of work. They have to make the agonizing call that removes a child from their home. They have to put them through unnecessary trauma, but they don't want to risk the child's emotional and physical safety in the home. Social workers are often the "bad guys," certainly for the parent whose children are being removed.

Social work is a demanding, low-paying, and mostly thankless job, so to all of the social workers who might read this book I say, "Thank you." I see your long hours, I see you agonizing over the safety of a child in your caseload, I see you after the tumultuous interaction with a parent, and I see you when everything you have done to try and keep a family together falls short. Please know you are seen in all of this, and also when you're not afraid to step in and make the difficult decision to place a child in care for her safety. You are seen working extra hours to assure that you place each child in the right home, in knowing this child and loving her, and in fighting for what is best for her and her family. I see your tears at the end of a long day, when you wonder if you are truly making a difference in the lives of the kids and families you work with, and I want you to know that you are. You are doing something when most of the world would sit back and ignore the problem. You are leaving a mark and making a difference in the lives of kids and families every day. Thank you, a thousand times over, thank you!

My family has worked with and been let into the lives of some amazing social workers. To give a voice to their passion and their experience, I want to share some of their stories with you.

Carson

Carson is a Licensing Specialist at our foster care agency. He works primarily with foster parents, which is where he excels and right where he wants to be. Carson has an adopted brother who came to his family through foster care; what his brother experienced is nothing short of bone chilling. Carson grew up with a front row view of the reality of foster care, saw a lot of unfair treatment, and was particularly struck with the differences in the way his brother lived before he came to their family and after. Carson said that he wanted to learn from those who lived differently than he did and wanted to make a positive difference in the community for them. Carson began his career in social work as an ongoing case manager working with kids and families. He had been told that this was the most difficult role in social work, but he felt up to the challenge. What Carson found was that it exposed him to more painful experiences than he ever could have imagined. Witnessing the effects of abuse, loss, drug addiction, homelessness, prison life, prostitution, and rape took a toll on his heart that he never expected. Seeing all of this pain and then being expected to be a diligent worker, keeping all of the plates spinning because if he dropped one it could mean a child getting hurt, was challenging. However, Carson will tell you this experience shaped him as a person and as an employee. He carries this life experience with him, and it helps him all the more in his current role as a licensing worker. Carson uses his unique viewpoint as a means to make a connection with the families he works with. He recently told me, "There is nothing like being there for a person who is in need. It requires a great deal of energy, intelligence, patience, and honesty. This work we do is important and isn't for everyone, but it is one of the most meaningful professions out there."

Lauren

Lauren was our first case manager. She brought Joy home to us and is still very dear to our hearts. She worked with us with grace and ease when we were novice foster parents, and she taught us how to navigate the world of foster care. I think in many ways we are still fostering today thanks to her and all that she has shown us. As a foster parent, you get to meet many case managers. It is not uncommon to have three or four on your child's case by the time it is complete. We have seen all types of case managers—the good the bad and the ugly—in terms of how they handle things. Lauren is one of the good ones, one of the best ones I can confidently say.

Lauren told me that she didn't have a sense of what she wanted to be "when she grew up," but she always wanted to work with kids. This is evident even now when she comes over for the monthly home visits and lights up when we answer the door with our little ones in tow. Lauren is the kind of worker who will stay at your house and ask questions to determine what a child needs, and even more so, will spend time with us so we can ask all of the questions we need answers to. No doubt Lauren was busy, and I'm certain she didn't always feel like she had the time to give, but we never sensed that from her. It always made me chuckle when she asked me if I had any other questions at the end of every visit, even after an hour of already answering a ton of questions. We have seen that this genuine love for and interest in the kids on your caseload is not a given with every case manager. In fact, I would wager that the vast majority of case managers begin with these wonderful intentions in their hearts, but they quickly become worn down. Lauren keeps her heart in the job by focusing on the things she loves about it and the rewards that come along with the difficulty. It's the amazing kids and people she has met and grown relationships with who mean the world to her and help her keep going. Lauren has said, "Witnessing the things these kids go through and seeing them turn it around and come out on top taught me so many things about myself and others, and I will forever be thankful for that."

Vanessa

We first met Vanessa when she took over for one of our previous case managers. To be honest, hearing that we were getting a new case manager was a relief because the previous one we had was clearly burnt out which became detrimental to the child's case. Vanessa will tell you that her career in child welfare was the most arduous job she had ever had. All the same, what we saw was someone who cared about people, and we connected with that. Vanessa struggled with the images of the children on her caseload who were distressed. She wanted to make a difference in the lives of kids and families, but she found that she wasn't able to help the parents the way they needed. You see, Vanessa has a history of substance addiction herself, and because of the responsibilities of her case manager role, she wasn't properly able to help the parents who struggled with addiction. From our vantage point, Vanessa was making an impact in child welfare; she was a detailed, caring, and concerned case manager, but for Vanessa, she still felt like she was missing something in her work.

Today, Vanessa is working with the inmate population doing substance abuse counseling, and she loves it. She explained to me, "I know how difficult it can be; it feels like the world is against you, bringing you down, and you are stuck in a cycle that you can't get out of. I also know it's possible to become successful and have a happy life after addiction." Vanessa was so lucky to have people who believed in her. They helped to change her life, and now she is in the position to be that person for others. As a foster parent, I struggle with a sense of failure if we don't see the lives of the kids and families we care for turned completely around. Yet Vanessa said, "If I can positively impact one aspect of my clients' lives, even if they aren't able to stay sober, that is some sort of success to me." I love her outlook that the final outcome is not up to us, and as such we cannot judge our success in the immediate moment, but rather we can celebrate the success of being there for someone. Doing what we can to help others, no matter the final outcome, is still a success. Vanessa has shown us that!

Social workers often go unnoticed in the world of foster care. They are the unsung heroes who answer the call because they love kids and families, and they desperately want to help others. They stay in the game when the going gets tough thanks to a great support network, just as the rest of us who engage in foster care do. Social workers also get a front row seat to the growth in those they work with to balance out the pain and brokenness they all too often witness. Based on the stories our social workers have shared, it's safe to say they expected to see growth in the kids and families that they oversaw. However, I imagine they didn't expect to see growth in the foster families as well. I wonder if they also expected to see the change that would happen within themselves. Engagement in foster care changes us all—everyone who is involved in this journey cannot help but change.

Fellow Foster Parents

"You have not lived today until you have done something for someone who can never repay you."

John Bunyan

We've all heard the stories and seen the distressing pictures of children in foster care who were abused by their foster parents— the very people who were supposed to keep them safe. It's revolting to me that anyone would become a foster parent and then hurt the child. Yet grace reminds me that while there is evil in our world, no doubt many of these parents identified in the media must have begun with the right intentions. Sadly, they steered off course at some point along the way. The negative always gets more attention than the positive, and this is something Kevin and I are trying to change. I am here to tell you that all of the foster parents I have personally met on this journey entered into it for the right reasons and want the best for the kids who come into their care. Foster parents navigate the messy stuff hoping to bring healing and wholeness to children and their families. It's a challenging road and a difficult calling filled with people with the best of intentions. Kevin and I have met some incredible foster parents on this journey, and I'd like to introduce you to a few of them.

Our dear friends Max and Cristy approached us one day wanting more information about foster care. These friends, who are like family, had spent a significant amount of time in our home interacting with Joy, and it unlocked something in their hearts. Kevin and I were thrilled to be on the giving end of advice since we were on the receiving end only a short time ago. This was the start of something, the first of many meetings we would have with couples interested in foster care to provide support and information about the process. Max and Cristy are the kind of people who see others in need and will stop to meet them right then and there to help them through their struggle. We have witnessed this firsthand, so we knew they would be fantastic foster parents. They jumped in head first, and without any prior parenting experience, they accepted their first placement of two children—a toddler and a baby. Watching our friends open their home and their hearts to these amazing little souls brought great satisfaction to us as well, and helping them learn the ropes of parenting often brought humor to the tough work we were all doing. Max and Cristy loved the kids, and they quickly learned to love their momma, too. Although they wanted deeply to adopt these kiddos, they knew that returning them home was the right thing for the children, so with tears and wounded hearts they supported the reunification of the family. To this day, they help this family—not only the two kiddos who were part of their family for a short time, but also their momma and the siblings who have come along since. It is one of the most beautiful blended pictures of love and support in foster care I have seen.

In a precious gift to their hurting hearts, Max and Cristy were offered placement of a baby boy who had spent all of his short life in foster care and who would need an adoptive home. Together, we celebrated the day he came home, and along with friends and family, witnessed the beauty of his adoption several months later. Melded together as an inseparable family of three, they give and serve together as a way of life. This mighty boy of theirs has learned to freely give to others just as his parents do, and he is one of the most kind and unselfish children I have ever met.

Max and Cristy soon began walking out a calling to move overseas and work with a nonprofit organization; this would require a big move and significant life changes. As they prepared, they received an unexpected phone call for a newborn baby's placement with them. This baby had a new case, and there was no assurance of how that case would play out. Our dear friends considered what

God had placed on their hearts and knew saying yes to this child could delay those plans. They could have responded no, and no one would have thought any less of them—after all, they were already walking out a call of God. They could have simply continued with the plan ahead, but that's not Max and Cristy. Our friends, true to their nature, saw a child of God who needed a safe place and took the opportunity to say yes. That evening, I brought them a meal and some supplies and saw the instant love they had for this child.

I can tell you that nothing has gone as planned with this little guy's case, and there have certainly been setbacks and roadblocks. There was a time when it seemed that saying yes to this child created a no for what God had placed on their hearts. Still, Max and Cristy never questioned their decision; they knew their yes to this child was a yes to God in spite of saying no to a different opportunity. Max and Cristy will be the first ones to tell you that in spite of the unknowns and setbacks, their yes to God and to this sweet child has brought them blessings greater than they could have ever imagined. Last week we witnessed our friends' second adoption, and Kevin had the priceless opportunity to dedicate their son at the family gathering afterward. As Max and Cristy stood in the courtroom that day, they articulated their great love for their son, his mom, and the God who created adoption as an act of restoration. It's real now; this chapter has come to a close, and Max and Cristy can continue on the journey they began years ago. They will cross an ocean and begin a new life giving to others, taking with them the experience of foster care and two amazing sons to remind them of what saying yes to God looks like.

We me Daniel and Lisa at the start of their journey, and they've now been fostering for three years. They have needed to get their license amended at least three times in order to be available for more children. They started as a family of four with two young boys, stepping into the unfamiliar, knowing they had a home and family to give to a child who needed it for a little while. Their intention had never been to adopt but to be a safe landing place while a family healed and was put back together. They were never intimidated by a child's story or background. Daniel and Lisa have a God given gift to see hope in and for the children who come to them, even with the most troubled backgrounds. I have seen these two fight for the needs and best interests of the children in their care and the families connected to them with absolute love and grace. They dive into the messy without a second thought because they know they can make a difference. As a result of their willingness to take on the challenge of the kids who need it the most, Daniel and Lisa have become one of their agency's go-to families for difficult-to-place children. This is a family who knows how to love, who is fostering for all of the right reasons. This is the kind of family we should see news stories about.

I also think of Katherine as a sage woman with a flowing crown of silver hair who has fostered half of her life as a single woman with little additional support. Katherine has been a foster mom to countless children and has supported their parents' efforts to bring their children home. Katherine has worked, managed daily care, cooked the meals, cleaned the house, and cared for children born to another woman as her own with no signs of stopping anytime soon. Katherine is one of the most humble women you will ever meet; she shies away from compliments about the years of care she's provided for kids in crisis and quickly diverts the attention away from herself. Katherine is a true gem, and there are dozens upon dozens of children and families who are whole and healthy today as a result of her beautiful, selfless heart.

There are people like Jon and Angelique who have moved three times to make more room to continue fostering. They are remarkable people who love first without needing all of the details figured out. They have seen children come and go and sometimes return to them. This couple has adopted nine children from various backgrounds and needs. They are "Momma Angelique" and "Daddy Jon" to the kids living in their home, and Auntie and Uncle to the children who have entered their lives and returned home to their parents. These two love the children in their home and the families connected to them.

I recently heard of a family who fosters only terminally ill foster children. That's right, they willingly open their home and their hearts to children who are dying. I cannot imagine the immense weight on their hearts that this family carries, but I do imagine that in spite of the pain they see and the tears they cry, their hearts are full, knowing that they are walking out what they are passionate about. They are a safe place for children; they are angels on earth escorting these sweet children to Heaven. My heart bursts with appreciation for this dear family. They experience heartache because these babies deserve to know they are loved. Thank you, dear family, for engaging in a way that I cannot, that many of us cannot, but God has graced you to do. Thank you for meeting a need that many are not even aware of and for giving your mended hearts to the next child who needs a picture of Heaven on earth as they travel to their final destination into the arms of their Father.

I can't tell you about the great foster parents we've met and leave out Julie and Daniel. This couple had already been engaging in foster care for years when they received a call about three children who needed an adoptive home. Without a second thought, they opened their hearts and their home to these children with the intent to provide that lifelong stability these kiddos had been starving for. They became a family of seven overnight. Two of their three children are twins the same age as one of their other kids, so they are now essentially raising triplets plus two other children. The road to adoption of these three was paved for them, but the road to healing and becoming a family has been filled with challenges. Their family grew overnight, but the trust did not immediately come for their children who had experienced years of hurt. Still, Julie and Daniel showed up everyday for their children and proved over and over again their commitment and their love for them. Daniel and Julie attended hours upon hours of therapy with their children. They are exactly who their children needed in order to learn what family is. Their foster license is closed now, but Julie and Daniel still want to be involved, so they volunteer at their agency and local nonprofits. The impact they have made on the foster care system is undeniable.

We met Fred and Roxy a lifetime ago when Kevin and I were serving in our first ministry position. Their kids were part of our Children's Ministry, and they were the kind of family who was always there when the church doors were open, volunteering in a number of different capacities. They were a great family then, and they are an amazing family now.

Fred and Roxy volunteered at a summer camp for foster children—this, incidentally, would also our first involvement with kids in care. Fred and Roxy saw firsthand the baggage that kids involved in foster care carry with them, and that they needed more than just one week at camp could provide. Several years later, with the support of their biological children, Fred and Roxy became foster parents, accepting their first placement of a teenage boy. They engaged in general foster care, always for teen boys who were traditionally difficult to find homes for, for six years without much lag in between placements. As is the case all over our country, there was a great need for foster parents in their county and especially for the kind of foster parenting that Fred and Roxy provided. This incredible couple quickly became a sought-after resource for their agency who began calling on them for consulting.

Then, God planted an even bigger calling in their hearts. They dreamed of starting a business which would allow them to be with the kids in their care full-time rather than splitting time and energy between the kids and work. God lined things up perfectly for them to take this big step, and they received one of the fastest approvals for the start of a program like this in their county. Now, eight months later, their program is full, sought after, and going strong. Fred and Roxy will tell you that the more time they give to the boys in their care, the better they do. Many people would be tired with little more to give (and to be certain Fred and Roxy feel this way at times, too), but they know that this is what God has called them to do, and with His help, they can continue to reach more boys in their community with love. Fred and Roxy, with the support of their family, have fostered fifty-seven teenage boys with no sign of slowing down. They have had some great success stories and some not-so-great success stories, but they have learned to measure success differently. Roxy recently said to me, "We are learning that our job is to make an impact, big or small on their lives. If we can show them the love of Christ through our actions and our words, that is success."

I could continue on with story after story of incredible foster parents, the commonality in all of them being love and deep commitment to showing children they are loved. It's unselfishly giving of themselves and their families for kids who will enter their lives for a little while, or sometimes forever. Fostering is allowing a caseworker to thoroughly examine your family in search of any skeletons you may be hiding. It is non-stop appointments, therapies, meetings, visitations, and court dates. Fostering is sleepless nights taking care of a child born to another woman, it's saying yes to one more child when your home is already filled to the brim, it's letting go of a kiddo you have loved as your own and sending them home to their family of origin because you believe in family. These are the people and the stories that should fill our news stations, magazines, and papers. This is foster care as intended. This is beauty. This is love.

OneHope27

"Start where you are. Use what you have. Do what you can."

Arthur Ashe

We started a nonprofit called OneHope27. It was built out of a passion and a desire to do more, to have an impact in kids' and families' lives, bringing them hope. When we began OneHope27, Kevin and I had spent years in Children's Ministry, not to mention growing up in the church, so we had a good handle on the "church world." We had spent several years involved in foster care and saw very little engagement between the local church in our area and social services, and we supposed that we could build a bridge between the two. Beginning with a small group at our Foster Licensing Agency, we started as a faith based recruitment initiative. We spent months getting together and dreaming about its possibilities, knowing that we needed to start small with what we could do. In the early days, we got involved in church events to bring awareness to our mission.

Before long, we were busy with church events and speaking opportunities, and a lawyer friend of ours offered to help us file our 501©(3) pro bono, which naturally upped the ante. As we walked out this process and put a Board of Directors together, Kevin and I were excited about where God was taking this ministry venture. We began to feel our passion shift from the ministry we were doing at church to an "all consuming, can't think, don't want to talk about anything else" passion for foster care. Kevin and I recognized this shift and knew we need to make the difficult decision to step down from the position at a church we loved. It was painful because it wasn't just a church. It was our home.

Embracing that decision was excruciating, and sharing that decision with our Pastor/Boss and everyone we loved at the church was not any easier. This church was our home and had been a place of healing for Kevin and me—a place where we became passionate about serving again after a difficult first ministry experience. We grew up here, not in our childhood, but as young adults. Our kids were dedicated and baptized here. Our best friends were fellow staff members, and our kids' closest friends attended the church as well. This place had become our whole world. Many tears were shed as we surrendered this life, this place that we so loved. If we hadn't felt so passionately about foster care, I don't know if we could've done it—walked away from what we knew and loved and head into the unknown. To aide us on this new path, we were at a church that "got it"—they understood the Church's role in foster care. When we stepped away from church ministry, there were dozens of families who were engaging in foster care by doing that "something" they could do, most of whom were foster parents with a beautiful structure of support in place. Goodbyes and changes are always hard, but we had our church's full support, and they had ours.

As with most things in life, we have seen ups and downs running a nonprofit. It's not always fun bringing awareness to people of the needs associated with foster care or setting up support for foster families. Sometimes nonprofit work is non-stop meetings, paperwork, and organizing tasks. Sometimes it's not yet having the funds or manpower to do a project you have a vision for. Sometimes it is just a lot of waiting. Foster care is such a large and complex system with many moving parts. For me, a dreamer, it can be challenging to rein myself in. I had so many ideas, and there were so many possibilities. Over the past few years we've seen more ministries and organizations rise up in our area to serve those involved in foster fare. We wholeheartedly support these organizations and partner with them as we can and as they need. It's a lovely thing to see different people from various organizations come together to serve the same mission.

Some can foster, some can mentor, some can support, some can donate, and some can volunteer but *everyone can do something*, which is one of the things we base our endeavors upon. When we have a new idea, it goes through two filters. First, we ask ourselves if it brings hope to kids and families involved in foster care, and second, does it help someone choose to engage in foster care who otherwise might not? We have set aside ideas that didn't pass the test, but we had to be careful about how much we took on.

Our longest running support is our "Placement Bag" project, which every child who enters foster care in Milwaukee County is eligible to receive. Each bag has a new pair of pajamas, a new outfit, socks, undergarments or diapers, and a toothbrush and toothpaste along with little extras that are donated to us. This provides all of the necessities to get them through the first night. I talk about this project quite often, and I wish we could show footage of a child receiving a placement bag on the most difficult day of their lives. It's a day when they have been removed from all they know and placed in the home of someone they have never met before. When a child just entering care gets to open a bag and see something new and just for them with a handmade card inside to encourage them, it brings the brightest smile to their face on an otherwise very difficult day. This project has brought hope to kids entering foster care and their foster families who may not have clothing on hand. It's also provided a way for so many people to do their "something" to help. They can donate clothes and pajamas, make cards, or volunteer to put together our placement bags. Some of those volunteers who got their feet wet in foster care by getting involved with our placement bag project are now actively fostering, which brings rich satisfaction to my heart.

OneHope27 has engaged in many other projects and events to bring hope to kids and families involved in foster care, from satisfying the wishes of children in care to most recently presenting a Job Readiness Fair for youth in care. It was another creative way to not only bring hope, but also provide a way for someone to engage in foster care who otherwise might not. My heart filled with joy as I witnessed the growth in the attendees that day, and as a result, we have committed to holding this support event annually. This fall we will roll out a support plan for moms of kids just entering foster care, another avenue where we can help bring hope.

Still, beyond the projects and the events is the great opportunity to share about the heart of God which foster care offers. Leading a nonprofit organization, I have learned that I cannot do everything. There is a strong desire to want to do it all, but doing what I am able to do well is what's best. We all want to make an impact in our world, especially when we find something we are passionate about. My advice is to do it—just start. Get up and get going. Do whatever it is you can, and dwell there. That is where you will find your "something."

Epilogue

"Learn to light a candle in the darkest moments of someone's life. Be the light that helps others see; it is what gives life its deepest significance."

Roy T. Bennett, "The Light in the Heart"

Having your eyes wide open to those hurting around you is a gift and a responsibility that challenges us and makes me want to help others see more clearly. I often have to fight frustration and disappointment when like-minded people do not see things the way that we do because of the experiences that we've had. It is difficult for me to understand how someone can love without fully seeing those around them and be driven to some kind of action. Compassion is defined in the Webster Dictionary as, "sympathetic consciousness of others' distress together with a desire to alleviate it." I would have everyone living out of compassion if I had it my way, but I often need to be reminded that not everyone's eyes have been opened in the same way. We cannot change how others see or what they see, but we can help shed light on things in the hopes that it begins to open the eyes of those around us.

We are currently contemplating what our future involvement with foster care will look like. Due to some of the needs in our home, it may be time to close our foster license. But it's a difficult call to make when foster care has been our passion for so long. Just the other day, an old family friend asked if we were taking in more kids. When I mentioned that we were considering closing our license, he said, "Oh, I thought you would be doing foster care for a long time." The thing is, it *has* been a long time. Kevin and I have been foster parents for the majority of our married life. We have fostered for over seven years, which is seven years more than the majority of the population has. Truth be told, I didn't foresee an end date. I had come to expect that this would be our way of life indefinitely. To come to the place of considering closing our license has been an emotional process. How does one know they are done fostering? Is what we have done and the kids and families we have and continue to impact enough? How do you begin saying no when you have said yes for so long and when there is still a great need to be met? Yet, we are not the saviors, simply people who saw a need and grew in passion as we walked it out, and others will come behind us to walk out the same passion. We are painstakingly aware that we can't turn a blind eye to what we have seen and what we have learned, and we wouldn't want to do so. The big question is, "What do we do with it all now?"

Kevin and I continue to be passionate about kids and families involved in foster care, yet we find ourselves desiring more and more to create change in families before removal is necessary. With first hand experience with parents who could not safely take care of their children and are without family support to help them, we know that someone has to step in to provide family and safety. Yet that same experience has also shown us that sometimes, in our privileged view, we look down on parenting that seems contradictory to ours. Perhaps some children who are removed from their home could stay if we recognized cultural and social-economic differences appropriately, and this breaks my heart. If one child is removed from their family simply because of the area they live in or the color of their skin or other socioeconomic differences, that is one too many.

The more Kevin and I become aware of the racial background and injustice that continue to be a reality in our country, the more we are forced to examine our role in it all. We constantly discuss how all of this awareness fits together, and if our response has changed . . . and if so, what does that look like?

In our friend Jason Johnson's blog, he calls foster care a river. This is his way of explaining that we are caring well for the kids downstream—the children in foster care, but we also have to move upstream to help the kids and families before they get in crisis downstream.[5] As we continue to engage in foster care, because engage at this point we must, I imagine we will begin to move further upstream. As we continue to live in community, we will love and serve there. We persist in building more relationships in our city with our neighbors across the street and around the corner, walking with eyes wide open to see the needs of those around us.

This is our story of foster care and some of the people we met along the way who opened our eyes and changed us. As we worked on this project, it's been our desire to provide a resource, and our prayer is that you have entered into these stories as you read and have experienced an eye-opening of your own. I challenge you to process what your role is, how you will participate in the world of foster care, or how you can support your hurting neighbors next door. It would be an honor to hear your story about how you began engaging in the hurt you see around you. #everyonecandosomething

Website: onehope27.org
Instagram: @onehope27
Twitter: @onehope27

---

5 http://jasonjohnsonblog.com/blog/developing-a-holistic-orphan-care-ministry-culture

Acknowledgements

I am uncertain what more there is to say that I have not already written. The words I have put down and the stories I have shared are real and they speak volumes. We might still be walking in ignorance and blindness to the hurt around us if it weren't for these stories, these experiences.

Joy, your story will always be sacred to me because you were our first experience in foster care. Often people comment on how blessed you are to have been brought into our family and every time, I reply that we are the blessed ones. You changed us, Joy. Your tenacity, strength, and love has forever marked our hearts and changed how we live our lives. Never forget, baby girl, that you are a champion, you are strong, and you can do anything you put your mind to. Don't ever let anyone tell you that you are less than that because you, my sweet child, are a Daughter of the King who has "given you a strong heart," as you like to say.

Dear Ivy, I see you and want you to know that you are loved. You are not alone, and you are worthy of fighting through the tough stuff to find better for yourself. Better is out there, believe me—believe in yourself.

Dear Rebecca, although we met in an unfavorable way and fought against you for so long, we grew to see you and to love you. I pray you continue to stand on your own feet, strong and secure and grow more every day in the knowledge that you are loved.

Bubba Boy, you are and have always been a breath of fresh air.

Thank you for being my sweet boy who assures me that I've had my share of hugs and kisses for the day. Never lose your sweetness or sensitivity to others. God placed that deep inside of who you are, and it is a gift. You are a gift.

My Hero, you have shown me what innate determination looks like, and your silly antics keep us laughing, for which we are all thankful. I pray you never lose that drive because it will take you where you are intended to go in life. I expect your silliness will balance out your determination as the years go on, and I can't wait to see how all of that transpires.

Amayah, when we see each other now it is not as foster mom and daughter, but as family friends. I am so grateful for that place in your life and for the incredible mommy and daddy who are raising you. I hope you know how many people have and do love you, and I pray that you continue to grow in that knowledge and in God's love. You are beautiful, you are strong, and you are treasured.

To my fellow foster parents, you have educated us and shown us the ropes of foster care. You have stood with us through the difficult times as only those who understand this journey can. Thank you for sharing your stories with us and with the readers of this book. Thank you for opening your homes and hearts to the children and families that come into your care time and time again.

Sweet Emalee, you were just a baby when you came to us, and now you are a big girl. You may not remember much of your time with our family, but we warmly remember every moment. Keep close to your sister; she will be your best friend for life because she understands your story like no one else can. She will be your champion and you will be hers.

We have had the privilege of knowing some of the best social workers. Thank you for showing up to a difficult job everyday.

Thank you for raising up novice foster parents like us and telling us that we can do more than we think we can. You may feel your job is thankless, but there are hundreds of children and families that have been put back together or put together for the first time because of you. You make a difference!

To our village, those mentioned in the book and all those I was not able to share about. We could not do this life without you. You sustain us, you encourage us, and you provide laughter and love when we need it most. Thank you for joining us on this journey in a supporting role. You have not only kept us going, but you have impacted every child who has entered our home through foster care with your love. Thank you to my sister for helping me express my thoughts as I wrote this book. I can not go without special mention of both sets of grandparents, our parents who love every child that comes through our door as their own and support us.

My Big Boys, you continue to amaze me with your acceptance and love of others. Thank you for still being with us, for still wanting to make an impact on kids and families involved in foster care even though it hasn't always been easy. My firstborn and second born, you are something special, you are important, and you belong. Thank you for being the best big brothers around.

Michael, thank you for the way your sweetness lights up a room. For all that you have taught me and taught your parents about strength. You are a light, dear boy.

Manny, I wish I could go back and re-write your story and bring you to our home right from the start. You are loyal with a heart of gold, and you stand up for what you believe in. As you enter this next chapter of your life, there will be hardships and hurdles to jump over. But we know you can do it, and you know we are always here for you.

Grammy and Grandpa, I wish you could meet these amazing children and families who have entered our lives through foster care. Thank you for raising my mom, and in many ways my dad, with hearts that see and love others. Your legacy lives on in your children and grandchildren, and I just know you would bust with pride to see us now. We miss you.

To our parents, all of our kids, and our grandparents, thank you for your constant support and love. Having extended family for every child who has entered our home is a gift to us and to them. Thank you for always being in our corner.

This book would not have come to fruition without my OneHope27 board and family. You are a constant source of support and encouragement for us. Thank you for your relentless support of our mission to bring hope to kids and families involved in foster care, and thank you for taking our story and turning it into this beautiful resource.

To my city, my home, you have welcomed me in with opened arms and have given me beautiful opportunities to see and love better. I feel more like you choose me than I choose you, and I am forever grateful.

Chelsea, thank you for writing a beautifully honest forward about your own experience with foster care. Thank you for the hope you are bringing to the vulnerable kids and families in D.C.

Thank you, Orange Hat Publishing, for making this dream a reality. Thank you, Shannon and Christine, for seeing the worth in these stories and encouraging me when I thought a dream had died. Thank you for helping me to believe in this project again.

To my rock, my strength, my calm, my comic relief, my human jukebox, Kevin. If I ever doubted that God knew what he was doing you are proof that He does. You are strong in every area that I am weak and you give me the drive to carry on when I have lost mine. The sheer fact that God placed the same passions in both of our hearts that we didn't fully understand or acknowledge fills me with awe. Thank you for being a willing participant in this crazy journey and for opening your eyes with me to see those hurting around us. I love who you are.